WHAT OTHERS ARE SAYING:

"Some books demand to be written. This is one. And it also demands to be read. Ignoring domestic abuse cannot go on. Authors like [Lindsay Fischer] are sounding the alarm and we should listen. Heeding the alarm isn't always easy because it forces people out of their comfort zone. *The House on Sunset* does just that. [Fischer's] writing is raw, emotional, and gripping."

— *Self-Publishing Review*

"At first glance *The House on Sunset* sounds like a novel of some kind (perhaps a horror story?), but in fact it is a memoir, and be forewarned—it opens with the author being brutalized in a savage act of domestic violence; so those who have suffered similar fates and who don't need a vivid reminder of such common occurrences should perhaps look elsewhere for their insights.

Or not: because this is ultimately a memoir of survival; and in order to get to the survival piece, the sources of violence and victim reactions to it must be addressed."

— Diana Donovan, *Midwest Book Reviews*

"It's not an easy read. You sit in nail-chewing anticipation of the unavoidable. "The House on Sunset" captures your visceral attention and demands to be finished. The book ends with Fina still breathing, but with her riveting narrative and compelling style, the reader's eyes are opened to the never-ending after effects of abuse. The book ends. The journey does not."

— Suanne Laqueur, author of *The Man I Love*

THE HOUSE ON SUNSET
A Memoir

LINDSAY FISCHER

Cover Design by Shari Ryan Edited by Justin Bog

Previously self-published as *The House on Sunset*, 2014

Note: This is a memoir detailing Lindsay's own recollections of events
in her life.
All names and places have been changed. Certain historic events and
locales are sometimes used
for atmospheric purposes. The events are related to the best of
Lindsay's knowledge and memories.

Lindsay Fischer
St. Louis, Missouri http://survivorswillbeheard.com

ISBN: 978-0-692-71135-4

For the man who loved me back to life

ACKNOWLEDGMENTS

To my friends and family: if this is all you read, I'm glad you made it this far. Reading my secrets must be painful. It wasn't easy writ- ing it, but because you came back into my life and showed me love, I was able to tell the truth. It's been a long six years since I left the house on Sunset, one full of heartbreak and healing. Thank you for being the frontline, even when I didn't want you to be.

To the counselors, workers and survivors at Safe Connections in St. Louis: The people I met through my time in therapy crushed the stereotypes of abuse survivors. I met introverts and extroverts, women with college degrees and others without. The thing we had in common? Our abusive pasts and our strength to overcome it. Thank you for crushing the ignorant stereotypes society presents. Thank you for showing me abuse knows no boundaries and people must be aware we're all at risk.

To the woman who believed in me when I told her I didn't know who I was or where I wanted my life to be six months after we met, my individual therapist: You won't take credit for saving my life but I believe you did. Sure, I had to take the first step (and I'll take credit for that), but you spent three years fighting demons with me. Maybe you're not responsible for me meeting my husband or being brave enough to leave one career behind to pursue another, but you were my constant, with me through every week. You will always be an invaluable part of my life. I miss you (but I'm doing fine on my own, living my dreams, feeling emotion when it's appropriate). This book wouldn't have happened without you, because I wouldn't be *me* without *you*.

To every survivor on this planet: may you find the strength to share your story when you want. Thank you for understanding me in a way others don't. We are bonded, and I'm proud to stand beside you: the men, women and children whose lives have been forever changed because of an abuser. May your strength guide you through life. You are the strongest people I know.

Abuse Statistics
According to Domestic Violence Statistics.Org:

Every 9 seconds in the US a woman is assaulted or beaten.

Around the world, at least *one in every three women* has been beaten, coerced into sex or otherwise abused during her lifetime. Most often, the abuser is a member of her own family.

Domestic violence is the leading cause of injury to women—more than car accidents, muggings, and rapes combined.

Studies suggest that up to *10 million children witness some form of domestic violence annually*.

Nearly *1 in 5 teenage girls* who have been in a relationship said a boy- friend threatened violence or self-harm if presented with a breakup.

Every day in the US, more than three women are murdered by their husbands or boyfriends.

Ninety-two percent of women surveyed listed reducing domestic violence and sexual assault as their top concern.

Domestic violence victims lose nearly 8 million days of paid work per year in the US alone—the equivalent of 32,000 full-time jobs.

Based on reports from 10 countries, between 55 percent and 95 percent of women who had been physically abused by their partners had never contacted non-governmental organizations, shelters, or the police for help.

The costs of intimate partner violence in the US alone exceed $5.8 billion per year: $4.1 billion are for direct medical and health care services, while productivity losses account for nearly $1.8 billion.

Men who as children witnessed their parents' domestic violence were *twice as likely to abuse their own wives,* than sons of nonvi- olent parents.

LINDSAY FISCHER

ESCAPE

MY HEAD WAS leaning against the cold cement floor where I landed. My ankle snapped when he threw me down the basement steps. The pain hadn't registered yet, but thick blood filled my mouth.

"You're weak. Try to get up again, 'Fina," he said.

I let drips of warm blood spill out of my mouth and down my chin. I wasn't going to give him a reason to continue beating me. I knew any sound would piss him off more, so I kept quiet and took each blow.

And then something changed. He didn't need any provocation to kick me again. I coughed up and gagged out more blood, trying to breathe through the pain of being slammed against the wall over and over. The tears fell slow and quiet and I laid paralyzed, breathing in the stink of mold-covered walls. A red pool formed just in front of my chin.

This was the day I was going to die. He was finally going to kill me. I was ready for it to be over, for him to rip away the aching so I could rest, buried in the earth. Maybe the undertaker would dress me in the black riding boots I bought for our second date.

"Do it, little girl. Move. I want to see you crawl."

I lay there, silent and limp, trying not to tighten muscles.

He kicked me again with his loafer, the winged tip lodging itself under my ribs. "This is why you don't refuse what I want."

Even the walls radiated silence, mute witnesses to the attack, unforgiving as I crashed into them. His anger and tone continued to rise; I curled my knees up toward my head and reached out a hand, a sign of surrender.

"You think you're so smart, don't you? Don't worry about talking, okay? I'll fucking make you squeal."

He wore his usual jeans and polo, and his athletic frame loomed over my wilted body.

I thought I could stop my own breathing before he beat me unconscious. Then I'd have some power over what was about to happen. But I couldn't hold my breath long enough to pass out. I couldn't force myself to erase the last minutes of my life, and that's when I knew everything he said was true.

I was weak.

I was immature and worthless.

I deserved the pain and suffering.

"You disgust me, bitch. You think you're so special. Thinking about the time I wasted with you – with a fucking whore – makes me want to kill you. You've ruined my life, so I think it's only fair you repay the debt."

Those were the only words I heard, but I knew he said more. He didn't know how to stop. "I'll make you squeal," he said again, clutching my throat with his calloused right hand.

I didn't need to force myself to sleep now. He was going to choke the life right out of me. In a two-bedroom ranch on Sunset, eighty miles north of where we met a year and a half before.

SURVIVORS

SURVIVORS ARE CUT from the same string: a strong, fully-committed and unwavering devotion to people who steal our hearts. As we unravel, we calculate how much more we can take. We never have an answer to that question, but we know we'll keep saying *one more try*. If this is the last time and we help, then the suffering was worth it.

I'm a survivor of domestic violence. I'm a survivor of a relationship with a sociopath. I'm a survivor of physical assault, rape, financial abuse, and brainwashing. I lost my house. I lost my car. I lost myself.

Survivors sacrifice our bodies and minds, our wallets and hearts, for the chance to save someone else. They tell us we're not good enough and we believe it. We're too ugly, too fat, too smart, too stupid, too much. Not enough. They dehumanize us with sociopathic skill so when we look in the silver-framed mirror above the sinks where we cry and puke, the person we see is unidentifiable, skewed by what we think are our mistakes and blemishes. (My therapist called it body dysmorphic disorder. I call it a physical manifestation of exactly how I felt inside. I had no idea who I was anymore.) And that's before we leave, or attempt to leave. The sad thing? Some don't leave, and help never arrives.

After, it's the same. Nothing looks, feels or sounds normal, whatever that means. We stare at the world, searching for remnants of things we recognize. Good things. Bad things. Anything.

We fight our post-traumatic stress disorder to go outside. (Mostly because we're guilted into it.) *Everyone has an opinion on how survivors should heal.* And as we round corners, we look back over our left shoulders then our right shoulders, just to be safe, certain our attackers aren't standing behind us. In public, we lean against concrete walls and touch them, stroking the rough, creviced surface to feel the safety of a structure.

People tell us what we should and shouldn't do. Bosses and

acquaintances tilt their heads slightly up and over as we walk past with drooping heads. This is the obvious contrast between those who survived and those who did not understand. We should be happy because we left. It's over. Honestly, (sometimes I doubt this too) they weren't worth the time and devotion.

On the bad days, we hurt ourselves. We rip towel racks out of the wall and slam them into our skulls over and over until our physical bodies hurt more than our minds. Most difficult, it's hard to know how to free ourselves from the guilt, fear, and pain. Survivors have days we're numb and not sure what's worse, feeling insufferable pain or apathy. Then we replace the towel rack so no one else knows we still suffer.

This process is appalling. The healing is just as hard as the abuse—another kind of pain. We're brainwashed. Then we have to try everything over. We don't know if we like strawberry or grape jelly. *Is it okay to have an opinion?* The lines blur between the abuser and victim. *Are these beliefs his or mine?* Maybe they're a mixture of both now. Any answer isn't real anyway, even if they were our own, we probably don't believe the same things anymore.

I won't lie about my journey: The pain didn't stop when the beatings did.

I still have days when it's hard to brush my teeth or go to the grocery store. Holidays make me anxious. I haven't been back to his hometown since I left that hot July morning, an hour after he tried to kill me on the basement floor.

It's been five and a half years since I left Mike, and eight months since I graduated from abuse therapy. In that time, I've read Lundy Bancroft and Brene Brown. I've watched TEDx talks from Leslie Morgan Steiner and Jackson Katz. I've researched. And read more. And I wrote and wrote and wrote.

Strange and bitterly obvious, it's difficult to live, strive to be good, in a society eager to ingest and quickly overlook what is painful and scary. Domestic violence is an issue many people choose to ignore. Not me. My life was forever changed because the man I fell in love with manipulated me and used his physical size, professional reach, and personal illness to strip me of my ability to live without terror. I can't escape questioning moments, simple to complex, if I'm being logical or driven by the nightmares left behind.

He treated me as though I wasn't human and, on some levels, I'm not anymore. Any clues I leave behind could lead him to me. It's not fair. But I'm alive.

I call myself a survivor.

Before the house on Sunset, I would've laughed if anyone suggested I'd become a spear-carrying member of this tribe. Happy to say I'm still here, and this is my story.

THE TRAIN

BEFORE THE HOUSE on Magnolia, David – my ex – stayed at my place every night keeping me warm. The apartment was my first home after leaving college and a sign of a new stage in life: adulthood. David still lived with his parents, and staying with me was a reprieve from his family. We enjoyed playing house, cooking and cleaning as a unit, but he'd leave for days at a time, sometimes calling to check-in without inviting me out. It was then I realized he wasn't committed, and since he never returned the words 'I love you,' I thought his problem could be solved by my generosity. To distract myself from the glaring hole in our relationship, I threw my heart into my classroom and independence, quickly buying a car and, then, my house. Keeping myself busy helped me avoid breaking things off, and I secretly hoped he'd – eventually – reciprocate the feelings I had for him. Either way, it was up to him to make the call. I had given him all I could, even paying for a week-long diving excursion in Hawaii. If we were going to make it work or end it, I wanted him to do the dirty work.

My year-long relationship with David was my shortest, a serial monogamist until we ended things and a few months into home ownership. One my twenty-fifth birthday, David took me to dinner only to unexpectedly tell me he'd been cheating on me with a girl named Lacey.

A comfortable booth along the side of the restaurant, a few moments of laughter shared by us, and then the candle's flicker showed me his quivering lip.

"I'm seeing someone else, and I love her."

"You mean you're fucking someone else," I said, sharing my perspective without considering word choice. Speaking before thinking was my worst habit, and it often got me in trouble with my family. But I wanted to know how far he'd taken this other relationship and stop overlooking the warning signs (his excuses for not staying the night). If he was breaking up with me, I wanted every dirty moment of infidelity laid before me so I wouldn't miss him.

"It's not like that with her, Sarafina."

"But it's just like that with me, isn't it?"

He turned away and looked into the parking lot without answering. Suddenly I realized I'd become the other girl.

Shit.

"We both know you deserve more than what I've given, and I can't lie about it anymore." Never making eye contact, he toyed with his glass of craft beer, turning it in circles.

"You're right. You've been a major asshole to me ever since I bought my house. I definitely deserve more, but you didn't think you could wait until after my birthday? Does she know about me?"

He threw three twenties on the table and grabbed at the closest server's wrist. "Can we get to-go boxes, please?"

"Thanks for the birthday present," I said, hoping it was the last insult I'd need to hurl his way.

"I really am sorry, Sarafina. I never meant for this to happen."

On the awkward, silent drive home, I decided I'd known it was going to end, but disappointment ached against my lungs as the truth surfaced with every inhalation. No matter how hard I worked at a relationship, both people had to be invested. Passing small districts in St. Louis as we drove west, I remembered all of the warning signs.

I was glad in an angry, righteous way that he'd cheated, and dumped me (yes, even on a birthday date) because the anger masked my loneliness. He was the obvious villain.

When he dropped me off at home, the cold settled upon Magnolia.

* * *

I bought Magnolia in the fall of 2007. It was fifty years old, owned by the original buyer and came full of pea-green and pee-yellow laminate floors. It also had an old furnace and the original rope-strung windows. At twenty-four, I budgeted to pay a mortgage on a teacher's salary. Twenty-seven thousand dollars made me feel like a Hilton, even though upgrading the house, the windows or flooring wasn't an option.

The cool air crept through the old windows making the entire house a breezeway. It was charming until the weather changed. As Missouri's winter thrived, I layered my clothes to make up for the freeze that choked my old furnace.

January 2, 2008, was a four-sock night on my scale. If I made it up to three pairs (a six-sock night), I turned the furnace up two degrees. That was it. I survived without warmth, and it was easier without insane heating bills. But the temperature didn't matter that night, an unknown magic coursed through me.

One I never felt again.

The train tracks ran straight through the old side of town, adjacent to my street, one block south of my house and visible from the front yard. The train's wailing annoyed me at first, but quickly became dependable and soothing, like warm tea on a painfully scratchy throat. Not long after I moved in, I found myself using train whistles to coax me into bed, where I kicked off extra layers of socks and let my feet breathe under blankets before falling asleep.

Independent living had perks and my rituals were one of them. I owned something. I made the rules. Since David left me a few weeks before, I had to learn how to stay warm without someone else's body pressed against mine.

I avoided the pain of loneliness by looking at online profiles of men nearby. I flirted relentlessly, hoping to prove to someone, maybe myself, I was worth more than David thought. With no desire to meet anyone in real life, distracting myself from the discomfort became a new nightly ritual I kept secret from friends and family. They'd inevitably tell me about my out-of-character behavior, and I didn't want to hear or see logic. Nope. I wanted to choose this.

At first, Mike was just another face on a site, another meaningless distraction. But the second we started talking on MySpace, I was sucked into a world that would become far more unforgiving than anything I left behind.

He wore a pinstriped suit in his profile picture. *Uva uvam videndo varia fit* displayed next to his name.

The grape ripens or gains color by proximity to other grapes.

All of it, his almost crooked smile displaced by a structurally perfect suit and tie, his pictures from foreign trips and the hope he was exactly the opposite of the last guy, intrigued me into charming him, so I wrote him a message about the wine he'd mentioned, my flailing

Italian arms and love of carbohydrates.

Unlike the others, he responded by the time I'd woken up the next day.

"It's not often a beautiful woman messages me on here. Nice to meet you, Sarafina. I guess you already know my name is Mike but your profile doesn't say you're a mind-reader, so I'm guessing you have questions.

Me too.

Here are ten of them to start, and then we can go from there. Ready?

His unexpected confidence filled my house while I got ready for work, and thoughts of his playfulness, coupled with mine, stuck with me through my day in the classroom. Email after email, we asked questions from templates. We tested one another, digging deeper with every reply.

Three weeks in, dark holes in our hearts and life stories surfaced. He told me about his two children and his struggle to maintain decent relationships with their moms.

I made some bad choices when I was younger, and even though I regret them, they both ended with beautiful kids.

I chased happiness when I should've worked on myself. Having babies with two women isn't great for dating (hello, red flag), but nobody is perfect. Baggage comes in different forms, but we all have it.

I haven't found anyone to date yet who I'm comfortable with meeting Blake and Savannah. Those are their names, by the way. My babies.

I told him about my heartbreak, a twenty-six-year-old boy who couldn't love a twenty-four-year-old girl who only wanted to feel validated and significant. Plus, my shitty, immature and cutting behavior. Reason to be mad didn't mean I had reason to be an ass, yet that's exactly who I'd become: the girl who kept people at a distance (or pushed them further away) by attacking them.

My defense mechanisms suck.

Our conversations led to daydreams of what he might tell me when the sun fell behind the city's west side. For the first time in my life, I fantasized about talking to a man. Not being held by him or kissing him, just talking. Already having dumped on him the plagues I'd carried through adolescence into adulthood, I was better able to harness the harsh language and self-justifying behavior I'd grown used to.

Can I call you? he asked the night before we met.

Sure, I said, typing my cell phone number into a message and flirting with the send key.

My memory of David, a true rejection, scared me enough that I needed to shake it off. I paced from the computer into my kitchen and wiped the sweat from my palms onto my thighs, leaving tiny beads of moisture on my jeans. Feeling tingles of adrenaline in my throat and nervous weight in my feet, I bounced a few times to be certain my knees didn't buckle.

"You can do this, Fina," I said aloud, staring down my bedroom door from the middle of the kitchen.

I charged the room and fell onto my bed, the mattress pushing back against my stomach and its static clinging to my shirt and the hair that grazed the top of the bed. Reaching for the mouse as the recoil stopped, I clicked send so I wouldn't talk myself out of it. Flirtation over, commitment engaged.

My phone rang before I sat upright, and I flung myself into a modified plank to spring back into a seated position. My long hair whooshed past my ears and blanketed my cheeks, sticking to the moisture on my lips and entangling itself every which way. I picked up the phone without a greeting, using my fingers as a brush to get the hair out of my face before speaking. As it stood on end, I groomed away the tendrils, licking my hand and wiping the saliva into my hair almost forgetting he was on the line too.

"Sarafina? It's Mike. Are you there?"

His voice was as strong as his writing and I wrapped it around my body, carefully examining how each limb responded to his calm confidence. Familiarity joined the conversation before I spoke, our emails making me feel like we already knew one another.

"Yes, I'm here." I twittered away from the receiver, a nervous habit. Yet here I was, acknowledging and hiding it without having to think.

"I hope you're alright with this," he said. "I know you haven't met anyone online before."

"Have you?" I asked because I was curious. A tinge of judgment must've been present.

"Whoa there, chick. Some of us aren't as adorable as you."

The embrace I anticipated lasted long into the night. In socks, I danced across the linoleum. The conversation filled every room with thick enjoyment before I headed outside for a needed breath of winter air against my hot lungs.

"I used to do that to, you know," he said, replying to my story about David.

"You used to cheat on your girlfriends?" I said, attempting to inject little bits of laughter through our mostly serious conversation.

"No, 'Fina, I used to keep people away by insulting them. It was mostly so I didn't get more hurt than I already was, but I think you know what you're doing."

He was the only man who spoke my language.

"I'm working on it," I said. "It's not like I'm proud. I got my mom's sarcasm and my dad's dry wit. Couple that with being Italian and I was bred into this crap."

Breathing and laughing and smiling, the world sparkled that night. The stars reflected off the snow so brightly the ground and sky combined somewhere undetectable. Standing outside, I watched snow flurries float around me, hovering in the night's magic. Then the temperature lost its significance. This man lit up my insides.

I was alive when I told him about my tumultuous relationship with my family, impenetrable by the freeze. Being the second child, I screamed for attention. But Bella, my sister, was birthed all kindness and likable submissiveness. She lived to make my parents happy, and I refused to speak until I was three, only grunting when they tried to communicate. That's how I got the nickname Stripe, like the water-born Mogwai from Gremlins. Only fifteen months older than me, she showed more emotion when my parents announced their divorce, and I took on the role of big sister without her permission. She never liked or asked for my protection, but I didn't know how to deal with her breakdowns any other way. Her emotion wasn't weakness, but I portrayed it as such. It was beyond grasp that crying could heal you.

She bawled after losing her virginity, telling my mom within twenty-four hours. I hid my sex-life until she called me out.

"I know you're having sex and I need you to get on birth control," my mom said over the phone. I was at my dad's house, my boyfriend sitting next to me on the couch. "We don't have to talk about it now, but acknowledge that you understand."

"I'm already on it," I said, and I hung up on her before my dad got suspicious.

This contrast between us grew along with us. Ashamed of the distance and lack of understanding, I hardly shared my familial truths with anyone.

Mike became my exception, accepting me for who I was: a girl just out of college, trying to find her place in the world, someone willing to take risks to find happiness.

I could hear the train's last call heading south down Interstate 70's outer road. With just enough time to give warning of the impending sound, I asked Mike to hold on for a moment while the train passed.

"Strange," he said. "I hear it, too."

Before I was able to ask what he meant, the train barreled through, our call unimportant to its route.

The sound echoed through both ears. Maybe I heard the train outside *and* through the phone line. To be sure, I pulled the phone away from my ear and waited for the next horn. Then, once the train signaled its approach, I suffocated my left ear with the palm of my free hand and only listed to the one against the receiver. The whistle was the only noise coming through, confirming what I'd thought. Letting go of my ear, the same sound filled my head from a block away.

Holy shit. He was close.

I stood in my driveway, my heart beating against my chest, pounding louder than the wheels screeched. I dropped my phone to my side and began looking behind me and down adjacent streets, jerking front to back so I didn't miss him. Then, spinning in circles, I expected him to show up, only stopping to stare at the train tracks in disbelief. Was he standing just beyond eyesight, spinning in circles looking for me? I couldn't see him, but his proximity made me forget everything else that should've mattered. My hair caught snowflakes that shimmered in my peripheral vision.

Finally, the disruption ended when the train moved outside the city, no longer clogging the line or preventing conversation.

"Where'd you go, gorgeous?"

I couldn't speak.

"You there? Hey, Earth to Bianco, are you with me?"

"Did that just happen?" I still stared down at the tracks as though the train reappeared. I was mesmerized, ignoring the twinkling of the ground and sky.

This.

This was the magic I wanted.

"Are you in O'Fallon?" he asked.

"Could I possibly be anywhere else?" My hand pressed into my head to keep the excitement inside.

"Sarafina, I need to meet you."

I soaked up every word and breath and tremor. The world around me stopped: we were the only things that mattered.

"You do?" I replied, emphasizing the second word with charm and curiosity. "Did you know we were so close?"

"I'm not sure it matters, does it? We're here now."

You can call it fate or coincidence or serendipity. You can call it whatever you want, but when you're twenty-something and the rest of your life's already in place, it feels like trying to solve an equation only lucky people understand.

I smiled again, channeling the appeal I left him with after our first email session.

"What are you doing tomorrow?"

MEETING HIM

I TRACED MY FOOTSTEPS footsteps between the bedroom and kitchen until heat rose from the linoleum. Rejected outfits, clothes and shoes piled up next to my bed, spilled across the floor. I didn't want to see him. But maybe I did.

Meeting Mike carried with it uncharted concerns, and although I often relied on logic, my desire - the *maybe* – brought warmth to my gut. I only intended to talk to him online and distract myself from my loneliness. How the hell would I explain any of this to my friends?

Fighting myself was useless. The train consumed me, the sight of it barreling through town the night before, the world frozen as I spun around to find him. His voice echoing behind my eyes.

"Are you in O'Fallon?"

I'd absorbed his words and they danced through me. Simple possibility begged me to stop thinking and start acting.

"Sarafina, I have to meet you."

His confidence, the calm certainty of his request, struck me as replicable.

When was the last time you allowed yourself to live, 'Fina?

The repetition of movement, pacing my house, allowed me to convince myself it was time to stop using my head and start using my heart. After all, if I boiled down the last guy I dated, I knew it would fail. David shared concerns about his fear of commitment, yet I convinced myself I could charm him into monogamy. In truth, he acted like he was committed to me for over a year. Then he met Lacey and followed his heart, and dick, into her bed. I was left with a losing mind game. This time had to be different.

Pursuing Mike felt like asking myself to forget about the bad I hadn't yet recovered from. *This guy wouldn't stay any longer than the last, would he?* The uncertainty of dating, the horrific moments of questioning myself flooded back. David broke up with me because I wasn't who he was looking for, but he was too chicken shit to tell me. The other guys who came before him, some more successful than others, left their own scars, but I knew I had to do it again. I didn't want to end up alone. I wasn't good at it, unable to cope with remnants of a childhood where I felt neglected, unappreciated and lonely in a house full of family.

Everything else in my life fell into place on its own without any guidance or direction. When I knew I wanted something, I went for it. My job was rewarding. I owned a home and car, and a washer and dryer. This, I felt, was rare for a single twenty-something. I didn't brag about it, but I was proud. Still, my seemingly strong exterior had one blemish: if I didn't allow myself to feel, to face fear and rejection and love anyway, I wouldn't have someone to share it with.

The train stared me down. How I could ignore its magnitude? It was black and strong, humbling my petite frame. *What do you want me to do?* I walked the path next to it, picking up shattered pieces of fear, heartbreak, and regret. The details, much easier to process one at a time, became less terrifying, and I knew I could make the journey to his office. Step one? Get in the car. Step two? Breathe.

I found Watson, my year-old rat terrier, curled up atop my granny's quilt on the couch.

"All right, little man," I said, bringing his black and tan face to mine. "Momma will be home before long. Hold down the fort."

Setting Watson down, I grabbed my purse and dug for my keys. I called out to Watson, "And quit acting like a cat, you little monster. You might be small, but you're still a dog." He barely lifted his head before sighing to acknowledge my departure.

I shut the door behind me and ran to the carport. It was a cold day, my skin prickling as the cold rushed over me. I stopped and stared, coatless, where I stood the night before, hoping the memory would stifle the fear. My nipples hardened. I was all goose bumps and nerves.

Once in the car, my fingers curled around the steering wheel and my breath stuck to the window. I stopped fondling the wheel and drew dreams into the spots with the heaviest frost, swirling them into semi-permanence like an Etch-a-Sketch. Tiny slivers of my frozen yard showed up in each stroke. Then I counted to ten, repeatedly, watching my defroster make it all disappear.

Earlier in the day, Mike gave me his address. I drove the route once already, knowing I'd never again be able to remain unobtrusive when passing in front of his office in a yellow Volkswagen Beetle. The two-block drive had ten streetlights, one left and two right turns. Three parking spaces against the tracks next to his office faced my house and I imagined parking and meeting him for the first time, the entire world inside my heart begging to be found.

* * *

Mike had the body of an athlete, thick, broad shoulders and muscular legs. I wanted to be near him as I stared through my rearview mirror at his dominating figure. He leaned against the antique brick building behind my car, arms crossed casually, waiting for me on the top step of the entryway. I hadn't realized it the night before, but as I looked at the empty train tracks last night, just after it left town, the lights from his building shone down my street. Maybe I'd seen him without realizing it, but it made no difference. There was no denying we were meeting now.

Today, his button-down shirt was masked under a hoodie. His black Oxfords and gray wool pants the only hint of office attire I noticed as he stepped off the entryway stairs and onto the sidewalk, waiting for me under the city's lamp. For the first time since we started talking, a face would coincide with a voice, (with written confessions and shared heartbreaks).

One walk across the street divided me and him from becoming *us*, whatever that meant.

I stepped out of the car and onto Main Street. I'd passed this place hundreds of times since I moved in, but hadn't consumed every brick slab and window like I was while I waited for traffic to break. When O'Fallon was first established, the four-story building was its first hotel. Now it was surrounded by antique shops and a small bar that served craft beers. Considered historic, the building was well maintained by its owner and filled with new offices. Lucky for me, Mike found it and built his business on the lobby level.

As I walked toward him, the light shined down and accentuated his tan face. Bright flecks of blond hair dotted his five-o'clock shadow. His thin, pink lips creased with experience and life, broke once I stepped onto the curb.

"Hello, gorgeous," he said, unfolding his hands and stepping toward me.

"This is weird, isn't it?" I asked, looking toward him and then dropping my eyes, both nervous and smitten with instant attraction.

He reached me on the second step, and stopped with only inches between us. Just the night before, we were perfect strangers. Now he stood in front of me, a person I had to meet. His ring finger lifted my chin so our eyes would meet again. A boundary I anticipated keeping, I didn't think we'd touch that night, but his gaze caught me off guard. His eyes were stunning, an icy, pale blue, promising answers. If I could only search them a little longer, I swore I could find anything I wanted.

"A little strange," he said, "but what a story." Mist flew from his mouth as he laughed before turning away. I watched his frozen breath dissipate into the air, particles of life falling around us. Hopping up the stairs, he opened the front door with his right hand, guiding me in with his left.

"It's cold, gorgeous," he said. "Let's go inside and warm up." The moisture from his breath against the frozen night stopped as he stepped into the office.

I'd always had nicknames growing up, Stripe or Fish (a play on my last name) or 'Fina, so him calling me gorgeous brought more belonging to our connection. The word filled me again, proving I had more space inside than I'd known. Every time he spoke, other parts of me blossomed.

I followed the strong line of his jaw down his neck and back to his shoulders before sighing. His skin pulled firm against his muscles. The unknown thrilled me now, instead of instilling fear that something would go wrong. Maybe this time, I'd get it right.

OUR FIRST DATE

HIS OFFICE BECAME our meeting place and I stopped in every so often after work. Always there, he made phone calls or met with his marketing advisor, John, who shared the office space. John often worked late, trying to earn more money for his growing family. I considered his faded jeans and fleece jacket his work uniform, and the opposite of Mike, who dressed for impromptu business meetings and lunches. They shared a similar build, tall and stocky. Every time I walked through the glass-paned door of the office, I looked through the first door on my left to wave hello to John before heading into Mike's office.

It was comforting to have someone else around when Mike took late-night calls from clients. When John left early, I eavesdropped on Mike's calls, fidgeting with my jean pockets while Mike watched me and listened to whoever was on the other end of the receiver.

John and I could talk for hours. Teaching fascinated him, and his questions became an outlet for me to get out of Mike's way while his phone calls kept him busy, and to show off my knowledge and passion without bragging.

"I eavesdrop on your conversations, too, you know," Mike said. "And I wish I could watch you at work the same way you can watch me here."

He believed actions showed more than words ever could.

* * *

On the last day of January, I packed my monogrammed duffle bag full of student essays and headed to the school's gravel parking lot. I placed the bag on the black leather passenger seat and flipped on the heater. As my windshield thawed, I flicked through the crackling radio stations.

The school was in a remote area and the weather determined which channels came through. Some days I could get a station for the forty-five mile trip to work, other days I switched between whatever the antennae could find. Just as the heated seat warmed my thighs, my phone began ringing from inside my purse.

The screen flashed "Mom" and I stared down at it wishing it would tell me why she was calling. It was unusual for my mom to call, especially at this time of day. She meant well, but she always shared her stress with anyone who would listen. I loved her, but she wasn't comforting. She wasn't the first person I told about my period and she only knew I lost my virginity because I got a UTI. I avoided conversations with her as often as I could, feeling more drawn to my friends and their families than my own.

I grabbed my iPhone and slid the bar to answer, exhaling until I emptied my lungs.

"Hey, Mom. What's going on?"

"Well, you know your grandma was at your house today," she said, the 'ay' sound abruptly cut off, withholding further words and baiting a reaction

I fell in love with the potential in every tiny room at Magnolia. The oak floors were hidden beneath orange and yellow calico shag carpet, but I knew I could refinish them once the house was mine. On the day of the closing, I drove straight from the signing to my new-to-me home and sat on the front porch, staring across the street at the elementary school children on their playground.

Buying a house was a good step for me. I wanted to prove I could be financially responsible and make my parents happy. They were hard to please and I sought ways to hear affirmations come my way, instead of toward Bella. On the day I closed on my house, I did exactly what was needed to hear soft words from both of them. A rare reprieve from being "the disappointment," I was the first to make an adult purchase.

"Yes, Mom. Did she paint the floor again?" I asked.

My grandma lived alone for as long as I'd been alive. Grandpa had ruined her for other men, leaving her with five kids to raise while he headed to Seattle to start another family. Without choices, she learned how to do everything he used to: home repairs and yard work included. In her own home, the same one they lived in together, she decorated the walls with constant reminders she could live without a husband. A pink hammer tacked to a wooden plaque. An embroidered, smiling teddy bear sat above the saying, "A woman without a man is like a bear without a bicycle," framed and hung in the hallway. My grandmother became independent because she had to, and she liked contributing to my new house and my liberation.

Grandma planted yellow and orange mums in the front yard; she bought Dollar Store curtains and painted the hallway floor – an old brown vinyl – Kelly green. All her own projects. All on different days. When she painted the floor, I came home and smelled the fumes before stepping one foot inside. Gone when I arrived, she had opened every working window and barricaded the hallway, then left a note. *"Painted the floor today. Hope you like it."*

It wasn't that I didn't appreciate everything. I just wished she'd ask. I overreacted a few times. And I'd called my mom to yell at someone who would listen. This time, my mom was silent, waiting for the right moment to tell me what went wrong. Each second passed as slow as the defroster warmed my windshield. Impatience, another gift from my mom.

"She let Watson outside today, Sarafina," she said.

I sucked in a breath and flipped off the heat, waiting for her to break the fallen silence.

"Well, he must have gotten himself free from his leash again, 'Fina. She can't find him."

Two weeks earlier, my grandma let him out unsupervised. I spent eight hours searching the surrounding neighborhoods, unable to find him. It was twenty degrees outside that night. I ran down streets, shivering in my hoodie while screaming his name. I knocked on every neighbor's door, praying they saw him. At three o'clock in the morning, I resigned myself to call the emergency line. If anyone contacted a shelter or veterinarian about a missing or found pet, they would have called the police. If they knew where he was, I'd be able to pick him up.

No luck.

Watson weighed eight pounds. It was too cold for him to be out overnight.

I cried in bed for two hours, wishing to hear his little whines and whimpers at the door. I thought of him stuck outside freezing to death in the frigid temperatures and I felt helpless.

I took a weeklong vacation to Jamaica for my best friend Ellen's wedding, so another day off wasn't possible. I cried as I pulled out of the driveway the next morning and headed to work. Ten minutes into my commute, a city officer called my cell phone claiming to have found my little man. I pulled off the highway at the next exit, called work to tell them I was running late and drove home to make sure Watson was safe.

The officer was sitting on the porch when I made it home. Watson's paws pressed into his chubby cheeks and he licked the tip of the officer's pudgy nose. When I made it to the porch, Watson climbed into my arms and did the same to me. The officer explained how he got cold that night and sat at someone's front door crying until they opened it. The little girls of the house, six and four, were so excited to have a visitor their mom told them they could have a slumber party, but explained the puppy would have to be returned to their owner the next day. When she called the police, they knew exactly where his home was, according to the description I gave the night before.

Two weeks later, it was happening again.

"Tell her she needs to get out of my house, Mom. She cannot be there when I get back." I hung up before she could reply. My dog was my life, the only constant and loving relationship I had.

Unsure what to do, I called Mike a week after our first meeting.

"Hey, gorgeous," he said.

"Are you busy?" I said between ums and uhs.

"Nope, it's pretty tame right now. What's up?"

Pulling out of the school's parking lot, my composure vanished.

"Can you run to my house and see if you can find him?" I asked, anticipating he'd say no. He'd never been to my house and the company kept him busy all day, even though he said otherwise.

"Of course. Tell me how to get there. I'm putting on my coat now."

* * *

Watson wasn't as adventurous that day. Mike found him in the schoolyard across the street minutes after we hung up.

"It's a little too cold for him to be out here right now, so I wrapped him in my coat and we're waiting for you. Drive safe." I read his text and let off the gas. Watson was home.

I pressed ignore every time my mom called. While I recognized none of this was her fault, she wouldn't understand why I hung up on her. Maybe sometimes I was bitchy, but she would use every one of my mistakes against me without questioning why I responded the way I did.

Mike and Watson sat in the same place I found the police officer two weeks before. I rushed toward them once I made it home. Watson's head was poking out of the jacket near Mike's chest.

"Thank you, thank you, thank you."

"You're cold. Can I come inside with you guys? Dinner is on me tonight," he said, directing me toward my front door with his hand pressed against the small of my back.

We were about to have our first date. He said we could go anywhere I wanted and what I wanted was a spicy tuna roll.

Both of us were wearing our work clothes. But we were hungry, and neither of us wanted to take the time to change.

Mike asked if we could stop by his apartment to grab a paper he needed to take back to the office. The excitement of our first public appearance subsided when the guilt set in. He left work to find a dog for me, and now he was missing crucial hours to take me to dinner.

"We can get dinner to go, Mike. You don't have to miss work to take me out."

I stared out of the old Audi's window, at the flood plain surrounding us on Highway 40-61. The criticism from my mother made it hard to feel excited, even though *we* were going to dinner. Maybe I behaved badly by taking Mike away from his work. Maybe I did act like a spoiled brat who only thought of herself. No maybe about it, but I can't be polite, kind, and generous every second of every day. It's all too much to live up to.

My mom was still capable of ruining my mood, even as a twenty-five-year-old on a date with a man who checked every box on my wish list. My defensiveness and agitation followed me through life and caused anxiety, yet nobody could pinpoint the root of my anxious behavior. An ongoing struggle, my parents forced me into therapy at seventeen. They thought my hostility and stress had to stem from something, but the therapist disagreed. I was doing everything right or, at least, that's what they told me. I was a normal kid with a big workload, and it was as simple as that.

My therapist also told my parents the same thing when they were called in to discuss my problems. After, they refuse to take me back or admit I was a problem. My mom had a different idea about my difficulties. I always had a feeling they came from her, though. My mom and her many opinions, animating teen-angst and fear. I knew it wouldn't be long before Mike resented me for the time I stole from him, just like what I thought my mom felt.

"What's going on in that pretty blonde head of yours?"

I stared down at my lap again. My goose bumps visible through my black, sheer tights.

"Nothing. I'm hungry," I said, turning back toward the window so he couldn't see the tears forming in my eyes. It was pretty stupid of me to be so upset about her. I should've known not to hang up. Gut reactions always got me in trouble.

"My mom is like that, too," he said.

I tilted my head backward, eyes toward the ceiling to push back the heavy tears. "I'm sorry," I said, looking back at him again. "I know it's ridiculous."

"Don't be sorry, and it's not ridiculous. I understand. I would respond the same way if I talked to her today. Funny how they can make us sense we're still children, isn't it? She's why I take my anxiety medication, even though she says I need it for other reasons."

We pulled into the parking lot of Zen Garden, a small Japanese restaurant in the valley.

"We'll stop for those papers after dinner. Right now I think you need a drink."

He jumped out of the car before I had time to respond. He knew exactly what I was feeling in that moment. I was thankful another person on the planet understood the dangerous reality of having a parental relationship like mine.

The restaurant was cool and quiet. A father and his adult son, the only other customers, silently ate octopus and eel sushi rolls in a small booth against the front wall.

Mike ordered two rounds of warm Sake shots, and I followed up with an Asahi chaser. We toasted to Watson and his adventures.

And then we had another one and toasted to our moms.

His face swallowed itself on the second shot, puckered from his eyebrows to his chin. "These don't get easier as you age, FYI," he said, blotting away the dampness on his unfolding lips.

"I'll take your word for it, old man," I replied, reminding him I was younger, an asset in my mind. A breathy chuckle slipped out as the food arrived. My sadness dissipated with every chortle, we ate and drank away the memories of my mom from earlier.

* * *

Savannah had Legos scattered across the carpet, and I hopped over a few. I wondered when she was there last, but it didn't matter. I didn't know what it was like to clean up after anyone but myself.

He had nice microfiber furniture and Van Gogh paintings around the dining room. The red of his couch pulled out the gold tones in *Café Terrace at Night*. I found myself wondering how he managed to put the place together with thematic colors that moved through every room, and I admired the outward maturity.

It only took Mike a few seconds to find the paperwork he needed and he was pushing me back through the front door.

"I hardly got to see your place," I said.

"That's a good thing. I forgot how much of a disaster it was. Sorry. I'm totally embarrassed right now."

Stepping out of the apartment, snow began falling just as we left.

"Seems like it's going to be a rough winter," Mike said.

I looked up toward the black sky, watching snowflakes fall around us, silent and slow. "Is that what you think?" I said, looking past the weather and, instead, thinking of possibility.

We spent the next thirty minutes talking as we drove the newly slick roads back to O'Fallon. He was going to get some work done and I would go to sleep. Mike told me more about his relationship with his mother. And he told me about the mothers of his children, how one saved him from his own immaturity by giving him his son, Blake. The other, well, he was trying to do the saving with her, but she gave him his daughter, Savannah, a blonde, round-faced spunky little girl.

He was vulnerable when he talked about his kids. A love so obvious made his blue eyes sparkle all the more, and I hoped a million moments like this one lay ahead. The fights with my mother slipped from my mind, never earning another second of our time together. He made me wish for better, stronger days when I, too, could articulate some of the biggest mistakes I made.

His story consumed me.

"Thanks for tonight," he said, leaning across the emergency brake. It was after midnight when we pulled into my driveway.

I fell into his arms as he put his left hand on the back of my head and pulled me into his chest. He smelled like Christian Dior.

"I need to get going. I'll be at work all night."

"I'm sorry," I said.

"For what?" His laughter filled the car with a final moment of our night's happiness. "You just gave me one of the best dates I've ever had. I told you things I haven't told many people, and we're both smiling at the end. Don't say you're sorry, gorgeous. Tell me we'll do this again."

A SNOWSTORM

THREE WEEKS LATER, at the end of a Midwestern February, the ground suffocated under icy manacles, and the freeze brought fantasies of canceled classes. Living in O'Fallon and teaching in small-town Missouri, roughly an hour down Interstate 70, proved challenging when Mother Nature misbehaved. Winter's debauchery extended my weekends. I hoped for snow days as much as my students.

I watched snow fall at the old, brick elementary school across the street, my living room still thick with paint fumes from earlier. I curled into myself on my microfiber couch, waiting for a text message revealing a cancelation of the next day of work. Watching snowflakes slowed my thoughts of school, but not of him. My mind congested from unexpected, unfolding happiness and hope as warm and smooth as dark roast.

I hoped for clarity and truth, for guidance and camaraderie. I hoped he was sitting in the office, staring down the blanketed street toward my tiny house. Above all things practical, hope came easy for me, an idealistic young woman who believed the world offered itself to those who deserved it, and dreams took me further into unrealized, augmented realities. I meant well, I dreamed big and I lived hard.

I'd seen Mike a few times since we found each other under the lights of his office building, but we misused plenty of time on the phone. His branch, the newest, required more attention than the branches filled with old money, so his father wanted him there longer than usual hours. Mike didn't mind until we wanted to fill the time together. Stacks of student papers sat untouched on my coffee table while we talked on the phone: I wasn't exactly doing my best at work either. Passion smothered me, waking up places I didn't know slept.

My iPhone vibrated on my knee, waking Watson. Unamused, he lifted his eyes to mine, sighed, and tucked his nose back in my arm.

"What's the verdict, little man?" Living alone gave me free reign to share secrets with my dog whenever I wanted. "Are we sleeping in or making the commute?" I looked out the window again, down at the ground, estimating accumulation. It wasn't the worst snowstorm I could remember, but plenty of inches continued piling on one another without any indication of a break.

"*Hey you,*" the text read. "*Haven't been outside in a while, but it looks like the snow is getting rowdy.*"

I smiled at the text, distracted and amused. Sometimes we don't volunteer for circumstance and sometimes we do. "*My dad says 40-61 is closed at the Daniel Boone Bridge,*" he said.

"*That highway you drive hasn't seen updates since Screech was a household name.*"

"*Should I risk it?*"

"*Reverse the roles. What would you tell me?*"

"*I'd tell you to come here. To stay with me. We'd double with Bailey's and hot chocolate.*"

He was as bold as the drink he promised. "*You'd probably reject the offer, but I wouldn't want you driving. Plus, I want to see you again...*"

I read the texts like a love letter, slow and breathy, pressing his words to my chest, asking my heart to suck in their marrow. He didn't wait for me to reply, and the anticipation of his words tightened my floor. "*Thanks for the setup, gorgeous. I'm big, clunky, and smooth. An oxymoron (score one for this guy). Think I could come see you tonight, at least for a little bit? I'll supply coffee, if you want. No worries about staying, I have a blanket and stuff in the car to crash on the floor here.*"

His face. His eyes and mouth came to me while I thought of a reply.

"*I respect your silence. At least let me wave at you. Open your front door and look down to me.*"

I pulled my pant legs off my painted toes and stood, stepping onto cold hardwood. The chill caught my arches and trailed the nerves to my neck. Electricity drizzled down my bones and pulled my skin tighter, my body trying to keep in the magic he released.

Outside, the trees wept darkness into an otherwise bleached night, and just on the other side of the train tracks Mike staged a stark contrast to it all. A silhouette, standing in the center of his office's window wall, flashed into the night, his left palm open and facing out, gesturing hello to me from a block away. Frozen there, his free arm switched electricity on and off. Darkness then light. Then again. The flashes stopped once he assumed I saw, and he stood like a mannequin in a storefront, confusing anyone who passed his office and knew they didn't have a window display.

"Cute, funny man. I'm down for coffee. And if you need to borrow blankets to take back to the office tonight, you're welcome to come here."

The final buzz from my iPhone had me convinced he would be saying he was coming over. Instead, my principal announced we'd be home the following day.

Thirty minutes later, Mike was on my doorstep with two Starbucks' coffees and a grocery bag.

"I ran to the bar next to my office. The owner's a friend. He said it wasn't the best bottle they had, but I'm not his best friend either. Guess he wasn't expecting a large turn-out tonight. Hope you like red."

Watson greeted him at the door the way he greeted everyone, with no idea strangers existed. His tan butt wagged side to side as he bleated whimpers of suggestion to his new friend. Mike handed me the bottle and simultaneously lifted him off the floor. Mike always laughed about his name. "Hey, Watson. Where's Sherlock?" he said. Watson kissed his nose.

I poured dry, curt liquid into my wide-mouthed wine glasses. We found ourselves staring out the window, drinking glass after glass of Cabernet.

"You're Italian," he said. "You gotta appreciate the dry reds."

The thick crimson drink calmed my nerves and pressed against my throat as it warmed my belly. The more I drank, the better, excited nerves flushed my skin.

I wanted him to want to kiss me.

Would our relationship be as strong once our physical relationship began? Fear contained my drunkenness as we finished the bottle, acting as a safeguard against myself and my impulses.

"You're welcome here, you know," I said, having spoken too fast for my mind to catch my poor judgment.

"Are you sure?" he asked, standing inches behind me. The whisper of his voice claimed me again and my rising regret vanished. "I don't want to intrude."

"The only problem I have is that you aren't going to fit into any of my pajamas," I said, shocked by my own forwardness.

"I can sleep in these pants. It's really not a problem."

His lopsided, subtle smile confirmed he'd stay.

Both of us wanted it.

The snowstorm built and crashed against my house as we hid under the damask comforter. I was strewn across his body, the strength of his arms apparent for the first time. He pressed his forehead into the crown of my head and we breathed slow, syncopated breaths. Enjoying the speechless moment, my round bottom lip fitted to the curve of his chin. It teased of kisses.

With snow pouring outside and the heat of his body intertwined with mine, I surrendered to the safety.

"I haven't properly asked you on a date yet, gorgeous. Waiting – even for a kiss – seems to be what you want, isn't it?"

Stunned by his ability to read me, I mimicked the crook of his mouth with mine. "You bought me sushi when you rescued my dog," I said.

"Doesn't count in my book." He pressed his lips into my hairline, parallel to the part. I was safe to sleep in his arms.

* * *

I heard a clanking from the kitchen when I finally woke up. The sound of the faucet behind it hinted someone might be up doing chores in my house, something I hardly did on my own.

I wanted caffeine.

I threw on some socks and a MSU hoodie before looking in the mirror. My hair unsalvageable, I pieced together a messy bun and smoothed the frizz with spit and a headband.

From the other room, I heard him yell, "Morning. I've made brunch. Figured it was too late for breakfast and too early for lunch. Hope you're hungry." His button down from the night before wasn't on my dresser or the floor, and I feared he'd look constructed and professional while I groomed myself like an animal.

"Be right out," I said, making sure nothing unfortunate grew on my face the night before.

As I turned away from the mirror, feeling slightly defeated by my appearance, I found him standing in the doorway.

"How is it possible you look so good without any effort? How was I so lucky to wake up next to you?" he said. "And most importantly, how do you like your coffee?"

My cheeks burned. For whatever reason, this guy was blind to my flaws. Self-consciousness felt immature and unnecessary.

"Blond and sweet," I said. "Just like me."

It was a joke I told since the day my grandpa said it to me. With few memories of him, the only thing I liked about him was his sense of humor. He left when my mom was twelve. So when my sister and I hit puberty, mom struggled to keep it together.

No shit, I guess. My dad, even after the divorce, spoke highly of my grandma and her courage. He told me about Skip and his departure. The situational irony wasn't lost on me. Skip skipped town and left his wife with five kids to raise on her own, thus wreaking havoc on the rest of our lives. Sometimes he'd show up, usually around Thanksgiving, and stay for a few days. We'd all change our schedules to be sure we got to see him, even though I'm not sure why. Still, he always made us laugh or complimented our appearances: he certainly wasn't unpleasant to be around, but he wasn't really family. My coffee recipe came from one of our holiday conversations, when he asked me what I took. It was nice to have a good memory, so I held onto it more than him.

Breaking me from my memory, Mike pulled out the wooden chair from my table. "Here. Sit down. I'll take care of the rest," he said.

We sipped coffee and talked about the day. Eventually, he stood and moved the dishes back into the sink, putting his cell phone and keys in opposite pockets.

"Think I can swing by to see you before heading home tonight?" Mike put the cup to his mouth and looked out of the tops of his eyes as he waited for my response.

"Yes, I'd like that. It'll give me a reason to take a break from grading that massive pile in the other room."

"Good," he said. "I like spending time with my girl."

Before I could respond, my front door was open and he was on the other side. He turned on the patio and stared back at me, smiling as if he'd just been told a secret. Just as quickly, he turned back toward the day and walked to his car.

OUR SECOND DATE

"YOU LOOK LIKE my girlfriend from high school," he said, as he opened the door for me.

"Please explain," I said, throwing myself into the passenger seat, unsure whether or not to be offended.

I hadn't seen Mike in a few days. His schedule picked up after the snowstorm and I gave him space to convince him – and myself – I wasn't needy. I missed him though, our relationship innocent and inviting, safe and fun. I liked his warm, consuming arms around me, and the comfort of laying my head on his chest. I wanted it to happen again. Soon.

I wore new black boots to impress him, having bought them for our second date.

"You're beautiful, gorgeous."

I let out a silent sigh. "So, your high school girlfriend was a total babe?"

He laughed as he closed the door. I watched his smile widen, illuminated by the headlights as he walked to the driver's side, his shadow passing over my front windows.

Once inside, "My sister and her husband are joining all of us tonight. I wasn't sure, but they're coming now."

My black stockings clung to my legs as I tried to pull at them. The group we planned to meet included other leaders in banking and investments, friends. I was already stressed enough by them.

"Is this a test?" I asked.

They would see I was four years younger with less money and success. I pulled at my black nylons again, trying to remember my redeeming qualities.

"I know this is technically only our second date. I told them that, too. Don't worry, 'Fina."

We were headed to Madrid, the popular tapas restaurant in

Clayton, a thriving area for businesses and bars. By day, the streets were lined with suits moving quickly from one block to the next, between the courthouse and title companies. But at this time of night, it was full of college students, businessmen, and young entrepreneurs, each looking to impress anyone who was there and would listen. I worked there one summer, at a title company, when my older sister Bella said they needed extra help, but I hadn't been to this bar yet.

Madrid gained a reputation for the best red Sangria in town, so everyone expected a wait. The kitchen cooked elaborate small plates of roasted red peppers and broccolini, everything smothered in goat cheese. The scent of baked artichokes and grilled chicken skewers filled the night air before we saw the restaurant, and the ambiance didn't disappoint. Intricate blue-and-yellow tiles lined the ceiling and the adobe walls were covered in red and green knickknacks. Overcrowded, people almost stood on top of one another waiting for their names to be called. I bumped my way through the foyer to our table, Mike pushing people out of our way as we passed.

"They're going to love you," he said, looking back at me and reaching for my arm. "And you're going to love the booze. We're this way," he said, leading me toward the long, corner table.

Beers scattered everywhere, the table was full. Greetings and uproarious laughter came from all sides. I wasn't the only one who liked Mike. A few guys in their late twenties wore sweaters and ironed blue jeans. Two other girls were at the table: one wearing a gray sweater with a hounds tooth scarf, the other in a pink fleece Northface. I guessed even the less professional looks cost more than my outfit, most of it from Maurice's. Once they finally noticed our arrival, the crowded table let out a synchronized welcome while other diners at smaller tables glanced at us.

"Don't expect her to remember all of your names." Mike rubbed my knuckles with his thumb in reassurance. "Guys, this is Sarafina. You can call her 'Fina.'"

The synchronized welcome happened again, arms shooting out and upward, beers clinking together and slamming back on the table. The girl in the fleece chimed in last, only tipping her beer in my direction once as she looked me up and down.

"Hi, 'Fina. I'm Alisa."

Alisa appeared to be the same age as Mike, but he told me she was older, so I guessed she was in her early thirties. She smiled faintly, her eyes glazed. I convinced myself she needed to see my dimples again, and I flashed her another smile, nervous her stony welcome didn't foreshadow the rest of the evening. She looked away without leaving me any room to respond.

"Ignore her," Mike said. "She's always mad at me for something."

He ushered me to my seat, turning me away from the awkward introduction.

"Thank you for being here," he said, his lips grazing my ear.

He pressed his lips against my temple, his hand gripping my side. My body slid across the chair easily and I froze again, waiting for him to whisper anything else to me. Alisa's frostiness no longer mattered. I was on a date with her brother, not her.

"I'm going to kiss you tonight," I said, staring down the table at the people I'd just met as they laughed and reached out for one another, their wrists covered in custom watches or expensive bangles.

SPRINGFIELD

MISSOURI STATE UNIVERSITY forced me to learn how to live and grow, so when I received an invitation to go back to Springfield for a wedding, well, excited, I relished the chance to revisit the home that created my best memories. After dating just two months, I wasn't sure how a road trip with Mike would be, but he agreed to go. I think more than anything he wanted to see MSU too, having spent half his college career there and the other half at another state school.

Anxious, I stood in my classroom staring toward the back, watching the minute hand crawl across numbers. Teaching felt unbearable. The juniors were loud, singing Colbie Caillat. Sometimes serenading me got them what they wanted, other times it only provoked me. Today I was giving them the last three minutes to relax and unwind after a long week. We all needed a rest. The winter still held on even though spring's warmth lingered just out of reach. It often scared me how excited I was to leave the classroom on Friday. I liked leaving school more as a teacher than I did as a student, especially when I had a trip to look forward to on the other side of 3 p.m.

Mike waited at my house until I got home, when we would drive through tiny back road towns to Highway 44, then continue across the state to the southwest corner. He had a key now, and was planning to move in once his lease was up. Weeks away from his move-in date, the trip to Springfield gave us the opportunity to test out spending that much time together. If we were going to be successful, this weekend couldn't afford any bobbles. The plan was to check into the hotel and spend the evening bar hopping my old haunts.

When the final bell rang, like one of the overstimulated teenagers ready for a weekend, I rushed to my car and drove home. Every Friday afternoon the highway congestion doubled my commute. Interstate 70 runs straight through the middle of Missouri and college kids traveling from Mizzou to St. Louis made the drive longer on Fridays during the school year. My bags weren't packed. Or at least not completely, so I was more aggravated than usual. I used the time to plan the weekend: drinks, sex, more sex, more drinks and a little dancing.

Mike sat in the living room with two pieces of luggage next to him.

"Don't you think it's time to get a luggage set?" he asked.

He walked toward me, carrying the larger of the two black cases. "Come on, babe, I just got my adult card with my first real job," I said. "Plus, a mortgage payment."

"I know. You're getting there." He kissed my forehead and I put my chin to his chest. He was warm, dressed in jeans and a sweatshirt for traveling. There was no hurry anymore. I wanted to stay pressed against his body the entire weekend.

"Let's go see the old hood."

* * *

We arrived at the Springfield hotel three hours after leaving the house. An uneventful drive, we stopped twice for bathroom breaks, when I smoked. Mike didn't smoke. He claimed it didn't bother him that I did, but I sometimes caught him brushing second-hand smoke away from his nose out of the corner of my eye.

We arrived at our hotel, entered a standard double-occupancy room, and threw our luggage on one bed. Then I threw myself down on top of the other.

"Are you tired? I told you I would drive."

I rolled onto my back, looking up at him as he stood over me.

"I'm okay," I said.

I lied through falling eyelids. It was dark out by the time we arrived. Mike wanted to go out and see downtown Springfield, sit in the square and watch the university students stumble from one bar to the next. "Plus, I packed enough clothes for a weeklong stay. I need to get some use out of my wardrobe."

I rolled back onto my stomach and pushed myself up on all fours. He was behind me, pulling me up toward him. I continued moving up to my knees with his arms still reaching, gripping my hips.

"Thanks for the invite, gorgeous."

He spun me around to face him. Holding my sides, his thumbs pressed into my hip bones, pulling me onto his body, our lips touching. And then again. And again. His five o'clock shadow scratched blush into my cheeks and chin, yet the heat of our skin felt cold and electric. Thrilled, early on, I froze when he touched me. Mike let go and walked toward his luggage, unzipping the front pocket.

I stepped off the bed and grabbed my black satin tank top off the dresser. I pulled off the T-shirt I wore for the drive and let the tank's fabric fall across my body. My hair stuck inside, so I lifted it out and turned toward where he stood before. He was behind me, waiting for me to find him there.

"I was going to wait until tomorrow to give you this, but I couldn't wait any longer. I hope you like it."

He reached around my neck and placed a sterling silver chain on my chest. A black sapphire pendant hung square between my breasts. I pulled my hair above the shirt, so he could lock the clasp. I flashed a perfect smile for a perfect present.

"You didn't have to do this. It's not a special occasion."

"But I did, 'Fina, because my girl should always feel special, no matter the occasion."

Five minutes later we were out the door. As our cab driver drove us toward the center of town, I remembered unmatchable moments of independence in this town. First we passed the RibCrib where I'd worked, just across the street from the original Bass Pro Shop: a highlight for locals and tourists alike. Then down the way, another job at the daycare on Monroe. Just after passing it, the campus where I learned so much about myself and who I wanted to be. That I wanted to be a teacher and help students survive some of the most delicate moments of their lives. Where I learned how to pack beer cans into a backpack so they wouldn't clink as I walked past the dorm's security desk. Where Chris taught me what true love was.

I looked across the backseat toward Mike. He was looking at me, a slight grin showing on his right cheek.

"I love seeing you this happy, 'Fina."

Before responding, the cabby interrupted, asking where we wanted to be dropped off. The moment passed without me being able to tell him how happy I was. How special his gestures made me feel. Every minute got better when we were together and even though it was only a few weeks away, I dreamed of the day he moved in with me. The nights we could laugh in bed without worrying about when the next time might be.

He was it for me.

We arrived at Ernie Biggs, the popular piano bar on the main drag of downtown. The line was out the door but I expected it, having spent many nights waiting outside the boisterous bar with half-drunk friends while the happy hour professionals finished their parties and made room for the college crowd. I grabbed Mike's hand and directed him to the back of the line.

"Wait here," he said, motioning for me to save our place while he walked toward the bouncer. The bouncer took three steps out near the street and waved me out of the line.

"We're in. And we have a table," Mike said, standing just in front of the door.

* * *

The next morning I woke up to an empty bed, the sheets and comforter pulled off to one side. Mike slept on the floor underneath them, between the bed and bathroom wall.

My head pounded. Mike's breath was the only thing I could hear around my headache. *It must have been a good night.*

I rolled across the bed and found an open bottle of acetaminophen on the side table. One of us already took a full dose. There was a half-empty water bottle next to it and I quickly polished it off. I was only wearing the necklace he gave me the night before. I laughed at how ridiculous I looked, naked with nappy hair, only wearing a new piece of jewelry.

Mike heard the ruckus and moaned on the floor.

"I'm not a college student anymore," I said.

His voice was muffled by the blankets. I quickly grabbed my boy shorts off the floor and sat up to put them on. The memories from the night before were as foggy as his voice, but I knew why.

"The damn martinis. That was the deal breaker." Mike laughed.

"I guess it depends on what you call a deal breaker. I thought the martinis made our night, or maybe just mine."

He was peeling himself off the floor then peeling my underwear off me again. I lay back on the bed to meet him.

"We have things we need to get done today, sir," I said. And I meant it. We were in town for the wedding and I hadn't bought the bride and groom a gift yet.

"If there is one thing I know, 'Fina, it's how to make the most of a few extra minutes," he said, looking up at me with his chin resting in the middle of my rib cage. I smiled, listening to his words and feeling his body harden on top of me.

My underwear fell back to the floor and he pushed his lips lower and lower, following my body as far down as the curves would allow.

Lucky for me, he didn't seem to feel too bad either. Lucky for me, the man really could accomplish quite a lot in five minutes.

* * *

My best friend and college roommate, Dani, met us at the hotel before the wedding. She and her boyfriend Hunter were in town for the same event and offered to drive us. She'd met Mike a few weeks before when he dropped in on our girls' dinner night. I wanted him to meet everyone as soon as possible and he said he missed me. They didn't spend much time together that night, but their previous meeting made the wedding weekend less awkward. She was excited I had a guy to bring with me, one who could talk to her boyfriend while we reminisced about our college life together.

The couple held the ceremony in a tiny no-name town thirty minutes south of Springfield. The winding roads were unmarked and we were lost fifteen minutes before the ceremony began. I was sure the couple wouldn't notice our absence, but I hated being late to anything. We found a one-pump gas station seconds after realizing we were late. Inside, a man gave us directions to the chapel. Mike bought Dani some Tylenol for a headache she mentioned earlier. If he was trying to earn points with either of us, he did. Hunter, however, gave him hell about making him look bad. We were back on the road soon enough, but realized we were too late for the ceremony when we pulled up to the church. The doors closed before we parked.

"What should we do?"

We sat in the car weighing options. We could walk in the church, hoping we made it in before the ceremony started, or we could drive back to Springfield, find a bar and be early to the reception.

We chose the second option.

* * *

I'd mailed back the RSVP invitation to the wedding in December several weeks before I met Mike, and when we looked for our place settings, I found mine. The cream card-stock name tag next to mine hosted a familiar name, but it wasn't Mike's. It was my ex-boyfriend's. *Fuck*.

I grabbed the tag before Mike had time to notice.

"Ready?" I asked.

"Following your lead, gorgeous."

As we turned away from the table, a familiar face from across the table – a smug high school acquaintance friendly with my ex – grinned and dropped his head to laugh under his breath.

"What was that about?" Mike asked.

"I'll tell you when we get to the table, babe."

The centerpieces stood taller than me, so I had to look around them to see Dani and Hunter on the other side. Thank God they were at the same table and we were near the bar. The hosts knew us too well.

I turned to Mike, who picked up beer on the way to the table, and watched him swallow his drink. "The place card had David's name on it," I said.

"Is that all?"

"Yes."

"Well, I was expecting something a little more dramatic than that. Like maybe the guy who was laughing *was* David."

Dani and Hunter heard the conversation and immediately began laughing. Mike winked, a sign of my unnecessary worry.

We enjoyed the rest of the evening, dancing and drinking until it was hard for me to stand in my black stilettos.

Our final cab ride of the weekend took us back to the hotel. Mike threw me over his shoulder and carried me to our room. My feet hurt from two nights on the dance floor. Without putting me down – or breaking a sweat – he took out the key, swiped the card holder, and entered the room.

He sat me on the bed and took off my shoes before turning around and pressing himself against me once again, my new necklace tangling itself into my hair as we kissed.

I couldn't remember life before him, how inexplicable the memory lapse was didn't matter. He was here now, unzipping my dress, as his thigh muscles tensed. My dress slipped off as fast as the loneliness I felt before him.

He lifted me from the mattress and placed me on top of him. I always noticed his strength when he picked me up, easily moving me where he wanted. My body tensed more and I let my legs slide over the edge of his hips. I pressed myself onto him and kissed him hard and deep, pushing him further into the bed as I regained my composure.

He wrapped his hands around my wrists and pulled me down again. I melted into him before I realized he was still wearing his clothes. We took turns undressing each other. Once we were both naked, I climbed back onto his lap.

The lights were still on. I could hear cars at the intersection of Battlefield and Campbell.

"Lots of little hiccups today," I said, staring down at his face.

"Yeah, well, they happen," he said. Mike grabbed my waist and pulled me forward then pushed back, rocking my body on his.

I remembered back to my drive home from work on Friday, how everything I wanted to happen did, and I never wanted to worry about making perfection again.

It was so easy with him. Wrapping myself around him and letting him move me around until I came. I was excited to continue this when he moved in to the house. We could have this every night.

SAVANNAH

I KNEW EVERYTHING about Mike's daughter before we met.

Savannah was only two, a tomboy who loved spending time at Mike's parent's farm in the town of Louisiana, Missouri. When given the chance, Mike took her in the Gator cart, darting around the vast land his parents owned. They loved stopping at the pond to feed the wild ducks. None of this happened often.

Ann, Mike's ex, Savannah's mom, a woman used to getting her way, often used Savannah as a playing piece against Mike. Or, at least, that's what he told me. She asked for clothes or additional money when it was his turn to see his daughter, and refused to let him if he didn't pay. Alienation is a cruel punishment. He hadn't seen his daughter in three months.

Mike and Ann met online too. He was working in Louisiana and dating in St. Louis. Ann was nothing short of beautiful. A competitive athlete. Because of her successes, he was drawn to her. She never told him she was deaf while they exchanged emails. It was only a few days before they first met she admitted she couldn't hear, so they brought notepads to dinner dates and sat in silence.

When Mike realized the relationship wasn't going to work, he tried to let her down easy. But she was stubborn and would drive herself the two-hour trip north to give him anything he wanted. He said she did this so he wouldn't leave. And then she was pregnant.

"I've got two beautiful blondes," he said, holding the steering wheel in his left hand and my thigh in his right.

I listened to him brag on our similarities for the entire ride to Embassy Suites.

He predicted Savannah probably wouldn't say a word, not even to him, that night. Talking wasn't a priority, as she only spoke ASL with her mom.

His mom, in a rare instance of support, pulled some strings and gave Ann a couple hundred bucks, a night away from responsibilities and the promise of an updated Spring wardrobe for her daughter. If there was one thing I admired about Mike's mom, it was the amount of time and money she gave up for her grandkids. It was evident she was capable of loving, but I was still foggy on how she chose who she wanted to support.

Mike's mom, his sister, her husband, and their two kids all waited for Savannah at the hotel. If Ann knew Mike was there, she wouldn't leave her with the rest of the family, not even for the money. So Mike and I suffocated under wrapped pink boxes in his car, waiting for the call to come up to the room and see her.

Mike stared out the window as cars zipped past on Interstate 70. Tulle bows crinkled and shook from his tapping foot. They were piled high enough to scrape at my chin while I swayed with his movement, listening to the traffic hundreds of feet from our parking spot, absorbing the nervousness around me.

"I am so excited to see my girl," he said, appearing regrouped and ready.

I never intended to date someone with children, but I didn't love him less because his kid wasn't written into my plans. I was excited to see him with his daughter. We often talked about her and how much he missed her. Not being able to see her much made it hard for me to understand whether or not he was sincere. If I had kids, well, I don't think I could survive three months without them. Still, life had taught me not to assume I knew everything about situations. My married friends had already proven relationships weren't as black and white as I wanted them to be. So this was just another example of life taking it upon itself to prove me wrong.

I smiled at him, attempting to reassure him of my support. "She'll be excited to see you too, Mike. Thank you for letting me come tonight," I said. And leaned over as far as I could to kiss him, still surrounded by boxes. He met my lips and kissed them, then breathed slowly as he kissed my forehead. Showing me his silenced phone, his sister's name lit up on the screen.

The cue we'd been waiting for. It was time.

"Get these packages off of me and let's go see your girl." But he wasn't listening, already out the door and walking to my side. He held the door open and unpacked my lap while I soaked up his gallantry.

* * *

When we walked into her hotel room we found Savannah sitting on the quilted comforter kicking her pink shoes against the edge of the bed. It only took a second for her to realize what was happening. Her daddy was there, kneeling on the floor, waiting for her to rush into his arms.

Mike put his hand on the back of her blonde head, just like he always did to me. He scooped Savannah off the floor, celebrating their first embrace in far too long. They didn't speak. He kissed her forehead and hugged her tightly, then released her to do it all again. Finally, he let her down so she could show him every gift she'd received.

"Savannah," he said, carefully signing the words while speaking them. He was doing this for my benefit because she wasn't listening, but I was content gazing down at his hands in understanding.

"I'm fluent," he said to me, after signing something I couldn't understand. It didn't surprise me, as he was smart, but it was something I didn't know.

"I thought you and Ann wrote on notepads," I said, remembering previous conversations about his relationship with Savannah's mom.

"We did, but after I found out she was pregnant I decided it was time to learn. Funny thing about having a baby who learns ASL as a first language: it's easy to pick up."

I watched them speak in their language and I knew it created a special bond. They spoke in private, even though the room was full of ears.

One sign repetitious, I wondered what it meant as they flashed it back and forth. His pinky, pointer finger, and thumb all extended, while his middle and ring fingers pushed down against the palm of his hand. Every time he did it, she looked at him like he had just unlocked her world.

"Mike, what's that sign?" I asked, trying to emulate what I'd watched them do all night.

He brought his right hand up to his face and recreated the sign in question.

"This one?" he asked.

"Yes."

"It means 'I love you'."

I smiled, realizing I should've known it was so simple.

"I love watching you two sign to each other. It's sweet."

He walked toward me, putting his hand on my hip while kissing my forehead.

"You'll never know how much it means to me that you met her tonight," he said.

I stood there, the warmth of his breath grazing my nose and lips for the second time. Every time he breathed into me, I fell further than before.

"She's beautiful, Mike."

Just then, I felt the warm grip of tiny little fingers. Savannah pulled me toward her, then toward the couch. Mike stepped back, unsure where he belonged in this moment, and watched his daughter draw me into her world.

She pulled me to the couch and climbed into my lap, putting her hands on my cheeks and then pushing away a strand of hair that fell across my forehead. We played. I spoke and she replied in sign, bringing Mike into the conversation as our translator. The rest of the family returned to the room after a quick pool session and started changing clothes to head out for dinner.

He looked through me then, and I knew he saw how much I loved his little girl. She did look like me, and I was once a tomboy, too—still a little rough around the edges. The moment her tiny fingers wrapped themselves around mine, I knew I'd do what I could to make her happy whenever I was around. All of these things flashed out of my eyes and toward her dad. Never having to speak my thoughts, we were also communicating without spoken words.

In the busyness of getting ready, his family didn't notice our moment. It felt like we were the only ones in the hotel room, and just as my heart didn't think it could get more full, the little blonde on my lap and her daddy by my side, he looked into my eyes and flashed me the only sign I learned that night.

I lifted my hand and replied the same thing.

* * *

Our visit lasted until midnight. His mom was ready for bed and we weren't invited to stay the night, everyone feared Ann would show up unannounced and find Mike. We left wishing for more time. Maybe Ann would allow her to come back sooner next time.

We got home late. Watson greeted us at the door, wagging his black tail tightly, shuffling out the door before we even made it all the way in. I followed him outside and stared up at the stars as he found a place to go potty. I felt lucky to be a part of their reunion.

Mike was in the bedroom when we walked inside. Watson jumped onto the bed and quickly put himself between Mike's legs then curled into a ball. "I'm so glad you saw her."

"I was just thinking the same thing," I said, lying next to him on my bed.

"I wish Blake could've been there too."

I immediately thought of his son, his first born who I'd seen only once at the office. Mike usually spent every other weekend with Blake back in Louisiana, where he lived with his mom, Mike's ex-wife, and I caught up on my grading while he was gone.

"I'd like to spend more time with him too, Mike. Still, I know he likes seeing you alone. I'm probably not much fun for a six-year-old boy."

"You were great with my girl today. Give yourself some credit. I think he's really going to love you."

He paused and looked over at me, putting his hand over my heart.

"I meant what I said before, 'Fina. I really do love you."

I smiled and placed my right hand over his, and used the sign I learned earlier that night to confirm I felt the same way. He leaned up onto his left forearm and slowly kissed me.

It was the first night I met Savannah. The first time I used sign language.

Most importantly, it was the first night we said 'I love you' to each other.

THE MOVE

MY SECOND BUSY year of teaching brought with it life-changing questions. With little support, prepping five different courses while also coaching the dance team didn't help my mindset. Overwhelmed by the attempt to better my skills and survive on my own. *Did I really want to be a teacher anyway?*

These thoughts surfaced as early as September and scared the shit out of me. To think my career choice was wrong shattered pieces of me I'd assumed would always be whole. But when David and I began struggling, I never shared my career concerns with anyone, so nobody knew how I resisted. A million parts of my first adult decision laid strewn across the classroom floor, I couldn't tell anyone why I was feeling this way, except – finally – Mike.

My boss was happy. My kids were happy. *Why wasn't I?* All I knew was nothing was connected anymore, and I wanted to sweep it all up and cement it back together before my coworkers found out how broken I felt.

Mike let me know he struggled working for his dad's company. He hoped to further advance his career and felt his dad held him back. I admitted my secret: my passion for teaching had diminished over the past year. Wavering, I wasn't sure if it was because I was overwhelmed or meant to do something else. Mike pushed answers from me.

"If you could do anything in the world, knowing you could support yourself, what would you do?"

It was a question I often asked myself. And one with an easy answer. "I would write."

"I read some of your MySpace blog posts. You should start that again. You're good," he said, validating my choice with a nod. His encouragement, three sentences in length, was all I needed to start scribbling, typing, and editing. Writing through my fears of an upcoming career change calmed me, and when I thought about who encouraged me to begin again, my love for him deepened.

"You can't make a living as a writer, Mike," I said. And I believed it.

"No, 'Fina, most people can't. But you can." His confidence in me was sexier than most anything I'd ever seen. But I was still unsure, fearful of change and inadequacy.

"Can we discuss something more fun? What about the roommate situation?" I stood up from the floor and spun around to greet his gaze, smirking like a child, circling where he sat. "I know this girl whose boyfriend is moving in and they've barely dated."

"Oh yeah?" he said. "What's he got to offer her that she couldn't have living alone?"

"Companionship. Mad bedroom skills. Dude can work it. Plus, his lease is expiring. I hear the girl is generous."

We gossiped back and forth about ourselves, role-playing through the question we'd both been asked by family members and friends.

"I mean, he's older, you know: a male cougar."

"So, how long have they been dating?"

I stopped and threw my hand over my mouth, stifling the words as they came out. "Just over two months."

Mike stood up and grabbed my waist, pulling me into him and putting his chin on the crown of my head. "They must be crazy about one another," he said. He kissed my part and tugged harder at my waist.

"Or just crazy." I pushed him away and flailed my arms and legs like noodles. But just as quickly as I joked, I pulled him back into our safe connection.

"We'll be alright. Right?"

"Of course, gorgeous. We'll be better than all right. We'll be living together."

* * *

Toward the middle of third quarter, only two and a half months after we met, Mike moved in with me and Watson.

Dark bags nestled under my eyes as State-testing season was in full swing. I came home later than he did every night, talking about state standards, pass and fail rates. All I wanted was a number: a percentage of my kids to pass the test so my job wasn't on the line. Every night he reminded me of a better option.

"You should be a writer, 'Fina."

Mike's dad drove in from his hometown and rented a U-Haul to help us get Mike's apartment packed and moved. That day filled with relentless rain and slowed his trip up Highway 61. We waited at my house for his dad to show up with the truck, and, finally, celebrated our new future with a glass of wine and a sandwich.

I had plenty of space for his couch and beds in my three extra bedrooms. Savannah was too small to climb the stairs every night, so we put her and Blake on the main level, in the room next to ours. I spent the previous weekend painting and cleaning, making sure we could move in their stuff and begin decorating. We were seeing both of them more often, something that made him happier than I thought possible. Between the move and his kids' presence, we were playing quite the family.

Mike's dad pulled in the driveway at noon and we left my house almost immediately. I could smell Spring – the sweet dampness on mud and grass – just before it arrived, and I only needed an extra hoodie and long socks to stay warm outside. We rode in the U-Haul and his dad followed us with Mike's Audi.

"You ready for this, gorgeous?"

I looked toward the passenger side mirror, my face blurred behind the streaks left by the morning rain. The highway passed behind us. "I'm more ready than I've ever been," I said. I grabbed his hand from the stick and squeezed it hard, sharing the electricity stuck in my fingers.

I'd never lived with a boyfriend before. Not officially, at least. In college, my boyfriend lived a floor above me in a one-bedroom apartment. My dad refused to let us move in together, even if it would save us money. I stayed in his apartment every night, only leaving to shower in my own. David practically lived at my apartment too, but he left frequently. Looking back, I knew why.

Still, before Mike, I always assumed I knew what it would be like to live with someone. Now I realized I had no idea what to expect. But it would be good, warm and comfortable, like how it felt when I was on top of him.

This was real now. We would share responsibilities and he was going to pay half of the mortgage (a reasonable price considering the cost of his apartment). He would come home midday to let out Watson. I saw us drinking coffee in the morning before leaving for work. I felt his arms around me moments before falling asleep. I heard him yelling at whichever sporting event was on that night. And I knew I was about to plunge into a part of life I hadn't lived yet. One I'd wanted since I was little, where a guy loves you enough that he wants you to stick around.

I kept thinking ahead to that night. Our plans. After we packed everything and moved it over, Mike promised to order take-out from the Italian restaurant down the road. There would be more wine. And then even more.

"You sure, 'Fina?"

Reality flooded in as he put his hand on my knee.

"Feels like I lost you for a minute," he said.

"I was just thinking about our night tonight. How you'll be my roommate once we make it to the house."

He smiled. "You'll be stuck with me then."

But I felt free. From trying too hard or second-guessing myself. I felt like the secrets I saw behind his eyes were no longer there and my heart understood. He made me want to try harder. He was going to help me reach every goal.

The rain dissolved into a mist. Gray fog hung two feet above the parking lot when we arrived at his Ballwin apartment. Rick and Mike jumped out – disappearing behind the thick air – and started moving the heavy furniture into the truck. Inside, I packed the miscellaneous items Mike forgot: a panoramic in Savannah's closet, wind chimes on his patio. A big picture guy, I learned to help Mike with the tiny details. They were, after all, what made things so special. Like the whistle of the train. Holding tightly to the memory, the metal barrels of his chime sounded, dinging and clanging against my chest.

Before long, I was watching the apartment complex blur in the rearview mirror. This was it. "Off to our house now," he said.

I silently celebrated that he was acknowledging me-and-him as an "us." It felt right to take this step, even though we hadn't dated long. He was ready to find someone who wasn't scared of his past (his kids), and I was ready to find someone who wanted a full-time commitment. When we found one another, we had no more questions. "Yes," I said, "it's ours now."

* * *

The boxes were piled on the couch and kitchen table, so we ate dinner on the hardwood floor. My iPod played on random while we dined, and I hummed through mouthfuls of pasta. Mike stretched his right arm in front of my mouth and clinched his fist, turning his hand into a microphone. I sang into his thumb, both of us swaying to Ray LaMontagne.

He pulled the microphone back to his mouth. "We're going to eat on the floor all of the time, babe," he said.

And I knew it was true. I grabbed back his hand and pulled it over, eager to report.

"Word," I said, looking down at our indoor picnic.

I wanted to say so many things, but I held them in for fear he might regret the move. That I'd appear eager or needy. I let him say everything I wanted to hear without providing much validation. Without interrupting, worrying about my own wants and needs, being more and more selfless and selfish, I listened as he told me about our future. I had somebody else to put first, a wonderful, new feeling.

He was going to help me find time to write. We would take the kids to the park on our weekends with them. I could teach Savannah to dance when Ann let her spend time with us, a much more common occurrence over the last few weeks, and I would help Blake with his reading homework when he stayed with us. Watson could sleep in bed with them. He would replace the green vinyl floor in the kitchen once I found a design I liked.

I finished my glass of wine, dreaming of the ways life was about to change for the better.

"You're going to be a writer, 'Fina," Mike said, standing and grabbing Styrofoam food containers off the floor.

Mike cleaned up the mess from our dinner while I sat on the living room floor, wishing he'd come into my life sooner and knowing he was everything I needed. He was thoughtful, funny, complimentary, and patient. He was also my brand new live-in boyfriend.

* * *

Tryouts loomed. Spring break was still too far off. I was exhausted, and the only time I got away from my job was when I was sleeping. My dreams grew louder every night. Mike could feel them when I laid my head on his chest, a smile breaking against and warming his skin.

"Writing isn't exactly the way to pay bills," I said. But Mike always reminded me he had a company, and his company needed a writer. Plus, Craigslist writing jobs were always posted on the site.

"It's possible," he said, "as long as you're willing to piece together a decent salary."

By the end of third quarter, my teaching contract always showed up in a sealed manila envelope, now only weeks away. Every time my mailbox was empty, I was relieved I still had time to think. I raced to it at the beginning and end of classes, dreading the thing I'd overanalyzed for months would become a reality: I would have to make a choice.

During sixth hour, with my juniors finishing a group discussion over *The Things They Carried*, the principal waved me into the hallway.

"We need to evacuate the students. We've had a bomb threat. You need to make sure nobody exits to the parking lot. Turn away every student and send them to the other end of the building. The bomb is in a car."

Until I experienced this, I assumed I would panic. I was in high school when Columbine happened and all of the school shootings that followed were also on my radar. I realized the possibility would manifest itself, that I would face a tragedy like those other tragic school shootings, emergencies, bomb threats, once I decided to become a teacher. All teachers talked about the big *What If?*

Worried, I walked away from the principal and returned to tell my students to put away their work.

"We'll talk more about the assignment tomorrow. Until then, take your books with you. There's going to be an announcement and we'll be heading outside."

The message came just as I finished speaking. The students didn't have time to ask me questions. I clutched my purse as I walked out of my classroom and stood blocking the hallway that led to the parking lot. My mentor teacher stood with me, explaining the protocol for searching the students' bags before letting them leave the building.

"C'mon, Ms. B. My car's right there." The upper-class students tried to convince me they should be able to leave.

"Sorry, guys, the school day isn't over yet."

Scared, students stared at us, some rolled their eyes, as we asked to inspect backpacks before ushering them to the other end of the building. Others just wanted to leave. Mostly, the school was eerily quiet and calm, static, and the silence made me realize this wasn't a drill.

The students cooperated and we had the building locked down in less than five minutes. The fire department and police officers stood just outside of my classroom, prying open the trunk of an old white car. Once we were certain every student was outside, the principal released the rest of the teachers to manage the student body. They were huddled together near the football field, some of them in tears, while others laughed, excited to be missing a class. Once the smiles began fading, it was clear the students knew more than I did.

I stood near the gate, verbally pushing back the stragglers who tried to sneak out. I didn't want to be near anyone. The realization started to set in: my school could be the next sorry place on the list of tragedies. I watched as the authorities towed the car away, the trunk pried open and flailing. Murmurs began. Students identified who owned the car.

"It's Denny's car!"

Denny was arguably one of my favorite students the year before, and I was certain he wasn't a depressed, anti-social loner bent on murdering his classmates. His writing was some of the best I'd seen from a seventeen-year-old, naturally inquisitive, always asking higher-level questions, someone who expected difficult answers. Beyond that, he was a regular kid struggling to learn about life and relationships. Denny didn't connect with much of his family, claiming they didn't understand him because he wasn't into the farmer's lifestyle. Secretive about his goals, he harbored dreams of leaving the small town to become an engineer. I helped him sort out his dreams even after our year together ended.

Once the students left the building, the staff walked back through the gravel lot around the brown trailers, our makeshift classrooms. We passed through the main hallway into the tiny, old library for an emergency staff meeting where we learned an anonymous caller accused Denny of bringing a bomb to school. The police arrived to investigate and found pieces of an antique rifle in his trunk. They arrested Denny next, and took him to the county jail. The principal was certain this would lead to his expulsion, but she was unsure of the legal ramifications. She promised to keep us updated and thanked us for our professional demeanor during the lock down.

I sat in my plastic chair for fifteen minutes after the rest of the staff left. Every word spoken was painful. Every word stuck.

Again, I found myself crying on the way home. Shaking in disbelief that the boy I knew from class could've wanted to hurt anyone, wondering if teachers in other school buildings across the country felt the same fear and pain after their favorite student shot someone. I didn't sleep that night.

Mike tried to console me, holding me until the moment he left for work.

"It'll be okay, 'Fina."

But it wasn't okay.

How could I've been stupid enough to allow someone into my heart without completely knowing them? I created explanations to relieve anxiety, knowing they probably weren't true. I had no escape from reality now. Denny was gone and I couldn't help him. I couldn't repeatedly allow his lonely pain into my life. Something told me this wouldn't be the last time I dealt with the heartbreak now linked to the teaching profession: fear.

I questioned my career path before Denny was arrested. Now it felt obvious I wasn't cut out for the job.

"You should be a writer, 'Fina."

Mike's words stuck with me through the rest of the semester.

The judge sentenced Denny to a juvenile detention center for six months. As my principal predicted, he was expelled.

"You should be a writer, 'Fina."

I wouldn't recover from this so easily, if ever, and I knew my teaching career had come to an end.

My contract paid out over twelve months, so I would have three more paychecks coming while I looked for a better position. Mike's dad agreed to hire me part-time through the summer. I had three months to figure out how to make money as a writer. Worst-case scenario, I would find a part-time job waiting tables to supplement the income from Mike's dad's insurance company.

I was going to make it work.

A MONTH AFTER HE MOVED IN

"WHAT THE FUCK, 'Fina? Your dog pissed on the floor."
I was sitting on the bed in my room, trying to finish my first writing assignment for a new job – a fifty-page real estate marketing book. I stared at the blank page in front of me as Mike moaned complaints in the kitchen, hoping he'd be kind enough to take care of the mess this time.

"I stepped in it, 'Fina. I'm taking my socks downstairs."

I heard Mike stomp into the basement and turn on the washing machine. It seemed impractical to start a load of laundry because his socks were wet, but I was learning to choose my battles. Impracticality didn't seem to matter to Mike anymore, and he started surprising me with ridiculous requests soon after he moved in. Sometimes demanding, he asked me to clean up dinner after him or expected me to sit in silence while he took business calls. Sometimes he woke me up because he didn't want to take the dog out, even though he was awake.

No matter what he wanted, he always found a way to make me feel guilty if I questioned him. Plus, his requests weren't difficult tasks, so it seemed easy enough to oblige instead of arguing. I set the laptop on my bed and looked over at Watson.

"You can't tell me when you have to go potty, buddy?"

Watson sighed and fell back asleep, his exhaustion and apathy evident. Since Mike moved in, Watson started marking his territory. At least that's why I thought he was peeing in the house. His demeanor changed, too. Watson – a little over a year old – was less energetic now. He put on three pounds in a matter of months, and considering he weighed only five pounds before, he'd practically doubled in size. I tried to be kind to him, change his behavior through encouragement and kindness. I failed, obviously.

I wondered if Watson could feel the difference between me and Mike. *Maybe it was something like little man complex?* I felt bad for my dog. Watson used to be so active, playful, and tough. Now he was just a chubby little thing who liked me to carry him around.

I grabbed the paper towels off the kitchen counter and sopped up the mess. Mike's footsteps gained strength as I sprayed the floor with deodorizer.

"That dog is gross and is ruining our house. How would you like it if I peed on the floor? Would you still think I was cute?" Mike said, coming into the kitchen from behind me.

"Mike, it's already clean. It's fine. He's still a puppy." Although I was saying this to Mike, I was justifying his behavior to myself. I felt guilty about Watson's new demeanor, even though I wasn't sure where it was coming from. This was his second home. Plus, I hadn't trained him well, took the time, since I moved, although I tried. Coke cans filled with pennies and taped shut. Kenneling. Puppy pads. You name it.

I looked up to find Mike standing near the entryway to the living room, facing the wall. His belt was open and his pants hung off his hips.

"What are you doing?" I jumped off the floor, shocked by what I was seeing: an adult acting like he was about to piss on my freshly painted walls. "Hey. Stop the shit, okay?"

"What? It's not cute when I do it?"

I stood in disbelief as he pulled up his pants, zipped them and laughed, walking out of the kitchen. But as soon as he walked away from the door, I crawled across the floor to see if he actually let loose in my house. He didn't. Thank god.

"Next time I will," he said, laughing from the other room.

* * *

When I returned home from work the following day, I found Watson tied to the porch railing. Mike's car wasn't in the driveway.

Watson saw me pull in, his butt swayed back and forth with a fast, hard tail wag. I picked him up. His body shivered against my chest, sending little tremors through me as I tried to unlock the front door. It was a cold day in April. Too cold for him to be outside. I wrapped him in a fleece throw and put him on top of the couch to warm up before dialing Mike's cell phone.

No answer.

I called the office.

"Babe, I just saw your call on my cell. You need to wait for me to call you back."

"Are you aware that you left my dog outside in the cold?" I said.

"Well, it's nice to talk to you, too, 'Fina. Fuck."

"Well, are you, Mike?"

"Yes, I am. I was trying to be sure neither of us came home to a mess. I figured he'd be fine outside. He's not a baby, 'Fina. He's just a dog. It's really rather offensive how important you make him."

I squeezed the phone harder, looking over at Watson fast asleep on the couch. Not long before, I sent Mike to my house to save Watson because my grandma left him outside in the cold. He knew how mad I was. He saw how upset it made me. He also knew Watson was important to me; how could he find this bad now, try to turn the situation around on me?

Knowing I wouldn't respond well to seeing him tied up in the front yard seemed obvious. Watson's leash was only long enough to get him to the edge of the landscape, so he either sat in the bushes all day or on the freezing concrete. Neither option was better than leaving him inside.

"Who am I talking to right now? You're aware he's my dog and I love him, right?" I said.

"Are you seriously wasting my time with this? It's a fucking animal and I don't care if he stays outside for three days. That's what animals do, 'Fina. I don't want to fight and I'm busy. I'll see you later."

I only managed to get out his name before he interrupted again. "Maybe when you have kids you'll realize a dog isn't important," he said.

"He's important to me, though."

"Then I guess the best we can do is disagree. I'll be home late tonight. Watson can sleep in the bed until I get there. I bought a kennel today. I'll move him into it when I get home."

Speechless, I stared at the living room wall and waited for him to finish talking. We never talked about a new kennel before. I wouldn't have been bothered if he'd asked—well, maybe. If I knew he cared about my dog things would be different.

"I might not have kids, but I do have a dog. He's not yours, and you can't dictate where he goes."

This had to be about Watson peeing on the floor the night before and now my dog lived in danger because Mike didn't think I trained him well enough or because his socks were wet. Clearly, it wasn't because he was trying to help him – or me.

"We'll leave him in the kennel when we're both at work. He won't pee in it because he has to sit there all day."

"What's this about, Mike?"

"Babe, 'Fina, you can't be mad at me."

Mike tried to reassure me his decision and purchase were rational, but I wasn't convinced. This was the same guy who acted as if he was going to piss on my wall the night before. Who didn't lift a hand to help me and instead acted as if he needed to teach me a lesson about dog ownership. And parenthood, and marketing, and business.

Maybe I didn't have everything figured out, but I also didn't need to have condescending conversations with someone who didn't listen.

I did though. In part, my anger came from his lack of communicating the problem. If he became this bothered, I would've tried something else. He had no right to make the decision for me. We lived together. We weren't making decisions together. "Look. This is best for everyone, even your precious Watson. He'll be a better dog after this."

"And if he's not?"

"We'll get rid of him."

THE END OF THE BEGINNING

THE OPPORTUNITY TO write lifted me through my last day of teaching, right up to the final bell. After a half-day, the kids were gone and I began check out procedures immediately. Watson had gotten used to his kennel, but I still hated it and wanted to let him out as early as possible, secretly preparing my grade books and classroom sketches earlier in the week. All I needed to do was turn in my keys and take my final walk to the back door leading to the gravel lot—get the hell out of Podunk. I stopped into several nearby classrooms to say my final goodbyes, but I couldn't hold back the smiles any longer, and some of my coworkers were pissed. They couldn't think of anything polite to say. My excitement was a slap across the face to someone who would always want to teach.

But this was an unashamed step toward my future. After only two years, I shouldn't feel apathetic toward my classroom. No tears shed. No regret followed me home. I listened to Patty Griffin on repeat, screaming lyrics until my throat burned. With the melody, my hands tapped the driver's side of my car, and I thumped my thumb on the steering wheel like a bongo. I shook the weariness of the morning out of my hair, tried to release built-up tension and anxiety before I got home.

The sunlight hazy, softening the view around me. May weather was fickle. A little breeze wouldn't stop our late-afternoon trip to the wineries. Five or six were lined up along Highway 94, surrounded by farmland. A dream, I craved wine and writing space.

Watson yelped from inside his cage, and I swooped him up as soon as I unlocked the metal latch. Mike turned the corner just as I turned for the door.

"I put him away so you didn't have to worry when you got home. Guess that was dumb. I should've known you'd want to kiss your little dude." He stood behind me, squeezing both of us into his arms.

"I'm letting him out one last time, then I'll grab what I need and we can head out." Watson nuzzled my neck on the way to and from the front yard.

Just before we left the house, I packed my journal, pen, and over-sized sunglasses, whipped my long blonde hair across my back and zipped my Northface fleece up to my collarbone. Without another thought of the classroom I left behind, I hurled myself into the passenger seat, cushion springs pushing hard against my butt.

"You ready, gorgeous?"

I looked over at him, still bouncing from the force of my entrance. "I've never been more ready in my life."

* * *

The winery was crowded, but once we heard the acoustic music past the gates, we decided to deal with the crowd. Each guitar chord echoed off the hills, music surrounding us from all sides.

"She'll take the Riesling. I'll choke it down with her."

"Thank you, sir."

"It's your party, 'Fina. You deserve it." He pulled me to his side, the cold bottle barely penetrating my jacket. "Let's bob and weave, girl."

The day drinkers swayed and stumbled against the uneven, rickety brick paths cut into the winding Missouri hills. We found a tiny two-seater table in direct sunlight, near the edge of the stone walkway that wrapped around the wine tasting bar, far enough from the band and drunks to concentrate. "A toast to the most talented girl I've met, and the future she holds—may we always celebrate your successes with wine and laughter."

Mike leaned over and kissed my forehead. I felt the heat of his breath graze my temples and found myself more drawn to him than the pen and paper. "I want to watch you work," he said.

So I sat and doodled circles and pyramids, winding curly cues turned into squares along the margins. They were blue and scratchy and soaked in ambition.

I clanked the plastic cup against the side of our table, repeating the flip in my wrist, willing it to put words in my head. The bottle was soon empty.

"Looks like we're due." Mike grabbed the bottle and walked to meet me on my side. "Don't overthink it. Just write." He kissed my forehead again, walking back to the tasting table. The wine and sun combined warming my gut. I unzipped my jacket, sliding it to the armrest and exposing pale, freckled skin. He rounded the corner with a bottle of red, and a cheese plate.

"Red, eh? I guess the guest of honor only gets to choose the first bottle?" I poked at his side as he walked past me, hands full. He filled my glass and divided the food between us. "I just got–"

"Did you get hot?" Mike said, interrupting me. I was going to tell him I wrote while he was gone.

"I always get hot when I'm with you." I laughed.

He stared at me, gripping the chair arms and holding his body up over the seat as he waited for my answer. A wrinkle crept around his eyebrow like a parenthesis. "Yeah, I got hot, babe. I didn't really want to sweat yet. You know what wine does to my sex drive. I thought maybe you'd bend me over once we got home."

I could make a sailor blush. A simple joke or sexual innuendo to bring him back, that's a mechanism I used when I needed his attention. He sat down and let out a laugh

The band started playing its version of "Fire and Rain" and we abandoned our table for the dance floor. He put his arms around me and I was full. His strong lead, intentionally moving me across the floor so as to avoid the other dancers. My head rested between his rib cage and chest as he whispered the lyrics in my ear. We swayed under the open sky. The band ended the song and he released me while I tried to grip his hand. Alcohol and sunshine, Mike and the valley, we were light years away from my old school. The sun set slowly as we walked back to the table.

I spent the rest of the sunlit afternoon eavesdropping on other conversations, hoping someone's words would spark a story in me. He laughed as I leaned back in the chair to listen to the couple seated directly behind us. "This is how the real writers do it," I said.

"Is that what you learned in your degree program?" he said.

"Among other useless facts, yes. Good writing comes from observing the world around you." I sat up, dropping the front chair legs back onto the stone below me. "Is that all right?" I winked at him, flirting away additional questions. "Did you hear me when I said I wanted to be bent over? I meant it." I drank the last of my cup, realizing we'd shared two full bottles of wine.

We watched the sky change colors, blue to gold and red and orange, until each guest headed out. My Northface jacket enveloped my body once again. Mike insisted he was okay to drive.

"Let's get you home, girl. We can continue the celebration there." And he kissed me again, until the parking lot cleared and we were safe to exit.

* * *

The drive home gave us more beautiful views of the Missouri sunset. The light reaching into valleys and over the tops of green hills as if everything were catching fire. I watched the final moments disrupt the ground, illusions of water breaking as we passed by. I thought of this moment, of all of it. Of us, and him, and me, and our dreams and identities together. *Why was I so lucky?*

"Can you get this for me, babe?"

My dreams drowned out the sound of his phone ringing, but his question brought me back into the car.

"Sure." I smiled at him, answering with a "hello."

"Who is this?" the caller said, an unknown voice. She sounded surprised, maybe even annoyed. "Hi, um, this is Sarafina. Mike's driving and asked me to pick up. Who is this?" I asked.

"Can you please tell him I'd rather have this conversation with him than with his newest fling?" Her words were all it took for me to know exactly who was on the line.

Amy. Blake's mom and Mike's ex-wife. Mike's previous warnings about her attitude rang true. If he'd checked the caller ID, he wouldn't have asked me to answer. Mike looked across the car at me.

"Who is it?" he said.

"I'm not entirely sure, but I think it might be Amy," I said.

Amy and Mike were briefly married, six months after they had a one-night stand that lead to a pregnancy. He told me his parents pressured him to marry her. His mom called him a disgrace to the family name, and threatened to take away his job. She even bought the ring.

The air in the car was thick. I sat listening to Mike affirm her thoughts with a few uh-huhs and one yes, while muffled screams came through the receiver. We were moving faster, his foot pressing harder into the pedal the longer she screamed. Queasy from blurred trees, our turn off the windy highway appeared as relief for me. I put my hand on his leg and pressed my fingers into his thigh, hoping he realized I was trying to get his attention.

Mike looked at me as I pointed toward the exit, nodded and made the turn while continuing their conversation. I stared at my lap and waited for the conversation to be over.

"Hang on, Amy. 'Fina was giving me directions."

Mike looked at me and mouthed 'thank you' before returning to the call. His slight smile broke the tension, but his request further agitated, and her screams grew louder as we rounded the next turn.

"Tell that bitch she shouldn't speak unless she's spoken to," was all she could get out before he hung up. I reached back across the car, putting my hand back on his thigh.

He brushed me away, like a fly from his dinner plate.

"Are you stupid?" he said. He was staring at me now, grossly ignoring the road ahead of us.

"Excuse me?" I said, searching for the humor.

"You shouldn't have answered the phone. You shouldn't have used that tone with her."

"I don't even know what to say to this, Mi–"

He interrupted me again, turning away from me and looking back at the road. "And you shouldn't have taken off your jacket. Are you so attention deprived?"

The rest of the ride was silent.

If I had checked his caller ID before I answered, we wouldn't be having this argument.

I was, once again, good at ruining everything.

WHO ARE YOU?

THE NIGHT SKY looked dark and threatening from the driveway, Mike put the car in park, dialed Amy's number and started talking to her again. I hopped out of the car and sat at the kitchen table with a final glass of wine, getting up to check the driveway for his car. He was still there, punctuating the conversation with wild gestures, fingers flying with disbelief, his silhouette slamming against the frame of the car.

I sat at the table again, looked and got up. And sat back down. Watson stretched on and scratched at my shin, begging me to put him on my lap. Over and over all of this happened, until, twenty minutes later, my front door opened.

He walked passed me standing propped up by the table and grabbed a glass from the kitchen cabinet. Turning on the faucet, he stood over the sink looking out the window into our neighbor's house, gulping down and then refilling his glass with water.

Quietly, without raising any commotion, he spoke to me for the first time in more than an hour. "You're a piece of work, you know that?" He put down the glass and turned around, leaning against the countertop with tightly crossed arms. "Amy is my son's mother and she'll always be a part of my life." He stood, leering at me across the room. "If she tries to keep him from me now, I'll blame you."

Tears dripped over my cheeks as we stared at each other. I dropped my head, set my cup on the table and began walking out of the room. "Who are you?" I said.

My back was only to him for a second before the walls began shaking and my decorations clanked against the paint. He catapulted himself behind me, his breathing labored and heavy. I felt his pinky first as he tightened each finger around my neck.

"Don't you walk away from me, 'Fina."

I stood still, feeling his grip tighten. He pulled me back into the kitchen, walking backward, and holding onto me as if I was his play thing.

"Do you hear me, little girl?"

Finally, as I allowed myself to feel the impact, I began to resist him.

"I'm going to sleep, Mike. Let's talk about this tomorrow." But he refused to let go and yanked harder.

"No, let's talk about it now."

The force surprised me. I needed to break away from him, and I flung my arm backward, flailing away our connection. He grabbed my hand midair and spun me around to face him. The moment thumped harder in my head as his screams were silenced by my confusion. I twisted my wrist and freed it, pushing him away from me. No thought. All action. I watched him stumble over the chair where I sat minutes before. I couldn't stop him from falling into the mudroom door. His elbow shattered a windowpane.

Blood drops spilled down the white door and hit the green and yellow-vinyl flooring, sprinkled patterns around the shattered bits of glass.

I ran to the sink and grabbed a kitchen towel while he regained his balance. I wetted it as he cupped his elbow with his other hand, blood pooling in his palm. I wasn't afraid of him then. Shock stung his face like his accusations on mine. I'd never loved someone like him, someone with complicated, stressful relationships. *Maybe this was something I wouldn't understand until I was a mom.*

He grabbed the towel, his fingers trembling, and slid on untied shoes before walking out the front door.

I swept up the glass, dreaming of hours earlier when we danced on the patio in the warmth of the daylight. He was what I needed to find, the calm. Yet here I was taping manila folders over a broken window, trying to heal the hurt by remembering the good. *Maybe relationships with powerful love had even more powerful fights.*

I opened the front door and stood in the yard, looking down toward his office. The light was on. His car was parked in front. At least I knew he was safe.

I turned to go back inside as I heard Watson whimper on the other side of the door. He must've been hiding earlier and probably wanted to go potty.

Just as I walked up the third stair toward my front door, a familiar horn blared from two blocks away. It was our train.

I grabbed Watson and led him outside, staring down the road toward the train tracks, watching each compartment pass by. It was hard to focus on any one thing, so I looked away, scooping Watson into my arms and placing him inside the front door.

The train was still passing when I lit my cigarette. I stared again, inhaling and exhaling, blowing smoke into the darkness. I didn't know what I did to make him so mad, but I knew I would never do it again. Whatever it was that started this, I would quit. I inhaled again, watching the cherry burn orange against the night. The train's horn grew distant, subdued, nearly out of O'Fallon and moving through smaller towns in the middle of the state. I watched as the caboose passed and disappeared, expecting to see the light on at the office. If I squinted hard enough, I might be able to see Mike sitting behind his desk, answering emails.

But the interior lights weren't the only ones at the office and as soon as I saw the lights atop of the police car swirling. I ran toward the building.

What had I done?

* * *

"He called us, ma'am," the police officer said. "He claimed he was worried about you and wanted us to head to your house."

"I don't understand," I said, staring at Mike's limp head in the backseat of the patrol car.

I wanted to see his eyes, to see the pure blue of them and imagine his soul looked the same: calm, reassuring, kind—this terrible nightmare to be over, Mike back the way he was. No matter how close I got to the car he wouldn't look up at me.

"He said you were suicidal."

We were standing in the middle of the road when the second cop car showed up. The young officer in the car left his engine running but stepped into the middle of the interrogation, arrogance surrounding him. His eyes scanned my body up and down, and I knew he was judging a situation – and people – he didn't understand.

"Are you suicidal, ma'am?"

The officer's words shook reality back into me. I stood in the middle of the road surrounded by red and blue lights while my handcuffed boyfriend waited in the backseat of a cruiser. Other drivers slowed down to stare. The cops stared. I was the center of all of it.

"No, I'm not suicidal. I don't understand why he's in the back of your car if he called you to check on me."

"Well, he called from here. Said you guys got into quite the fight. Then said you were extremely depressed and suicidal, and he wanted us to swing by your house to check on you. When we ran his name through the system, we realized he had an outstanding warrant for an unpaid speeding ticket. So now we're here, arresting him because of your fight," the second officer said.

The first officer on the scene chimed in, "Have you ever been involved in a domestic dispute before, ma'am?"

This was too much. He cared enough to call the police to check on me, but he also called me suicidal and mentioned our fight. Embarrassed in plain view, any of my neighbors could see me, I was face-to-face with two uniformed men who wanted to interrogate me.

"Domestic dispute?" I asked. "No, sir, I haven't. I've never been in trouble with the police. I'm a teacher."

I always assumed people in the most underpaid, overworked fields (teachers and police officers, in this case) had a mutual understanding: we did our job because we wanted to help, not for money. I realized that was a mistake. The second officer rolled his eyes.

Plus, I'd just lied to the police. I taught my last class earlier that day. I couldn't call myself a teacher anymore. The thought of being dishonest with the police, no matter how douche-like they acted, and everything else, left me royally fucked.

"This was our first real fight," I said, sobs coming up as I fought them back.

The first officer unlocked his car, reached in to his glove compartment and offered me a Kleenex. I kept looking back and forth from them to Mike, who still hadn't looked up. The first officer caught my attention by handing me the same tissue I'd just refused.

"You know, if there aren't any more calls within the next few days, this won't show up on your record. Unless, of course, it happens again. Then it shows back up."

I wanted to get home to wash off the salt. "When can I get him?" I asked.

"You'll have to pay for the ticket and post bail. He won't be registered at the county jail for several hours. Just keep calling. Once he's been processed, they'll give you an exact number."

I walked back inside the house and found Watson shaken from the fury he'd witnessed. I called the only person I could think might help at the time.

David.

"'Fina?" he said, unsure why I was calling after our last conversation went wrong. Early on, Mike told me it was important for me to forgive David for cheating, so I wrote him an email and sent it off, offering to meet up and discuss our breakup. We met at our usual restaurant, but the meeting was doomed from the get-go. He'd just asked Lacey to be his girlfriend, and didn't think I deserved an apology. It was fate, he said, that he found her. Bad timing didn't matter because he was happy. Unable to feel the same, I yelled at him and called him a dirty liar who deserved whatever bullshit his new girlfriend would eventually serve up. He was worthless and she was a whore.

Both of our new significant others felt we shouldn't speak after that. I cried into the receiver and tried to yank words from my chest. "David," I said before gasping. "It's Mike."

I knew my behavior from our previous conversation was immature and anger-driven. Now I was drunk, and scared, sad, and alone. Empty. "He. Oh God. I don't know what just happened," I said. "Slow down, 'Fina." David said. Lacey was screaming "Who is it?" in the background. It reminded me of Amy yelling at Mike earlier. *Don't speak unless you're spoken too* echoed throughout the house.

"I don't know what to do, David. I need help."

"'Fina, I can't do anything. You need to call someone else. Are you safe?"

"Yes, I'm safe. I think so. Oh God."

"Call someone else, 'Fina," he said. The conversation was cut short.

Lacey wasn't over the last time I'd called her a whore.

Staring at the bloody door, I gasped for air and slid my phone away from me. That was the most vulnerable I'd ever been on the phone and he still wouldn't help. If I was going to make it through the night, I would need to pull my shit together and think about who to call and why. How could I get us out of this without risking further embarrassment?

* * *

It cost $600 to bail Mike out. I had just enough money left from my previous check to cover half the cost.

I called his dad and explained the situation: Mike called the police because he was worried about me. He was worried about me because I overreacted when he questioned me for answering Amy's call. I pushed him into the window. His elbow was probably still bleeding. I only wanted to be honest. His dad offered to drive up in the morning and cover the entire bond.

"Has he been taking his medicine, 'Fina?" Rick asked. Mike took Klonopin for his anxiety when work stress was overwhelming. Once, he'd said he didn't think he needed it, but he took it to make his parents happy. *Keeping them happy means I keep my job*, he told me.

"Yes, I think so," I said, a bit unsure whether or not that was true. I couldn't remember ever seeing him take it. He didn't leave it on the counter. It wasn't in the bathroom vanity. It was just something he told me he did. Until then, I didn't have any reason to question it. Still, I kept lying for him to protect him from any backlash, something I never had to do before.

His dad was apathetic. "Just leave him in there, 'Fina. If you don't have the money I'll come out tomorrow and take care of it." He yawned. "Thanks for calling and telling the truth." His words twisted my gut. Leaving Mike in jail overnight seemed the worst possible option. Strange his dad seemed undaunted.

I called my mom and asked her to loan me the money. I lied to her and said he called the police because his neighbors at the office were being too loud and tied the rest of the truth in after that. (They ran his name and found the warrant.) Although hesitant, she met me halfway between our houses – about a thirty-minute drive – and lent me the money with a few obvious looks of disappointment but fewer questions.

I went straight to the gas station, paid for a money order and headed across the street to the police department.

He was in my car, headed home, in less than thirty minutes. We didn't speak. Once I parked the car, he walked straight back down the road, toward the office, without saying anything.

I cried in bed the rest of the night. Sleeping was usually easy, but I couldn't stop replaying every second of our day. *What the fuck happened?*

HIS RETURN

MIKE CAME HOME three days later, the first Monday of summer break. I ate Ramen, imagining normalcy instead of soaking in rejection at his refusal to come home. I searched for writing jobs online, distracted and shamed. Ramen and Facebook, it was like I hadn't grown up at all. My salary made it almost impossible anyway. Yet ghostwriting gigs were abundant online, so that was something.

It was the first time in three days I saw any silver linings. One job, just miles away from my childhood home, offered work in the office with other writers, writing books and copy. I twirled my fork around the salty, yellow-tinted bowl, grating the sides and clinching my jaw with the scraping sounds. If it was hard to finish my lunch, how could I finish the day?

Just as I pressed send, the tiny forward movement was caught by the front door creaking open next to me, like he knew I was trying to distract myself. I saw his key hanging out of the lock as the door swung open. Mike stood on the step of the porch, his head hanging as he looked up. He carried a hydrangea and garden rose bouquet, another bag of take-out swinging from his elbow.

My eyes burned yet I sat frozen on the couch. My Gmail account registered the sent message and I turned from him, closing the computer and pushing it to the side. The bag swayed in his elbow crease. I diverted my eyes from him and grabbed at the fork again. Apathy. It was all I could do to protect myself.

"I want to start by saying thank you."

I turned my fork in a circular, habitual pattern, between my thumb and middle finger. *He wouldn't win me over that easily.*

"My dad said he appreciated your honesty on the phone and we both hope we can work through this."

Mike reached into his pocket with his left hand, his right still clutching the bouquet. He pulled out a stack of money and placed it on the table next to my bowl, in front of my spinning fork.

"There's $300. He said you could pay back your mom or keep it to repay yourself. Either way, it's for you from him."

The silence in the room, no eye contact, was enough for him to realize I wasn't ready to talk about it. I destroyed the last few bits of my relationship with my mom by asking her for money to bail him out. I lied to his parents and told them it was my fault he was arrested. I did all of that for the sake of saving our relationship, yet I lost part of my humanity that day.

"I'm going to try very hard to communicate with you from now on. I'm sorry I was so angry with you for answering the phone. It's just that she doesn't understand I've moved on from her and she uses every little thing in my life as ammunition."

I looked up at him, desperately wanting his apology to continue. The last three days had been hell. I didn't sleep. I barely ate. And sometimes, when the pain and confusion were too much to handle, I threw up into my new toilet while holding onto the sink and wall, wishing I was a better person.

He looked down at me, placing his hand on the back of my head. The last time he touched me there, he was pulling me backward into our fight. This time he was gentle. He ran his fingers up and down the nape of my neck, massaging it slowly.

"I don't know where we are, 'Fina, but I want to go back to when you were happy. Maybe that was three days ago. Maybe it was a month ago. Songs reminded me of you and I want that back."

He set the flowers on top of the money and bent to kiss my forehead. Bills spilled off the stack and onto the floor. The room smelled like stale money and bad breath. I wondered if he brushed his teeth since he was released from jail. He gulped air and exhaled damp heat against my face.

"I do love you, Sarafina. I really do. I think we can make this work if we forgive each other. All I'm asking is that you leave behind whatever you're feeling and we move forward. I've already forgiven you. Do the same for me."

He stood and walked to the cabinet searching for a vase. They were in the third cabinet below the sink, but he didn't know. I wanted him to search, to show a commitment to something so I could buy time to think of what to say. I wanted to tell him this was his fault. I wanted to accuse him of being irrational and angry.

I wanted to be innocent, but I didn't know if I was and I wasn't ready to lose him. Every time I thought about how blameless I was, I thought about my family and our conversations. I thought about every time I was wrong in my life, and how much easier it was when I accepted my mistakes.

I dropped the fork onto the money, stepped over it and walked into the doorway to the kitchen. Leaning on the doorframe, I rocked forward and back, gripping my biceps for security.

"Where have you been sleeping, Mike?"

He fumbled through cabinets until he found the vase. Between us, the manila folder still covered the broken glass in the back window, a glaring token from the incident. Neither of us looked in that direction. He stared out another window, facing away from me. I stared at my arms, moving just enough to keep myself from remembering.

"I stayed at the office. There's a shower upstairs. It used to be a hotel, you know. Anyway, I had clothes in my car from my last trip. I just didn't know what to say to you and didn't want to ruin my chances of making this work."

"I've hardly slept."

"Let me take you to bed then," he said.

He put the vase on the table and emptied the flowers from their wrapping. They fell into place without needing to be rearranged, reminding me of how life should be: organic and uncomplicated. The office was so close, it didn't make sense for him to stay there all night without a bed – without food – unless he needed more time to think about what he would say when he returned.

"I don't know what to say, Mike."

He'd carefully orchestrated my exact words. "Then don't say anything at all. Let me take care of you, baby."

He lifted me off the floor and carried me to the bedroom. Watson jumped off the bed and ran into his kennel. I was too exhausted to think much of it. Mike laid me down on top of the covers. Then he shifted my body to the side to pull them out from underneath me. He covered me with the blanket and sat on the edge of the bed.

"I'm not tired, but I'm home now, and I'm not going anywhere. I'd like to take a shower and make some calls for work. Maybe take you to dinner after you wake up."

He walked out of the room before I replied. He was always so confident in his words and actions, knowing – without any hint of confirmation – I was his girl. He knew I needed him, his support and confidence, through my career change. He knew I made the choices I did because he gave me permission. And even if I wanted to reverse any of the decisions I made, he knew I needed to work for his company while I searched for a job. Trapped financially, I hadn't realized this until it was too late.

I heard the shower door slide in its frame and bounce off the wall. He started singing some church song I heard him sing once before when his mom told him she would fire him. "When anxiety gets overwhelming, you should sing. It stops the birds from nesting," he said.

I thought about my mom and how much she hated the idea of me quitting my job, regardless of my feelings. I tried to explain how unfair it was to the kids and me if I only stayed for the security of a monthly paycheck. *She chose what she wanted to hear.* The conversation tore us further apart and gave me something to prove to her: *I could do this.*

Mike's arrest only made my mother's concerns grow. Of course, this meant she and I grew even more distant. Although my mom wanted what was best for me, she was unable to communicate it in a language I understood. All I ever heard from her was, "Don't you know how this will affect me?" and "You are self-righteous and disrespectful." Comments like those made it easy to dismiss her concerns, especially when it came to leaving the man I loved. I'd always sought her approval, but I'd never received it. The truth of his arrest laid somewhere in the gray, and I wasn't entirely sure it wasn't my fault. If I didn't push him away, the call never would've happened. *But what would have?*

I heard him sing more lyrics and closed my eyes. I saw him standing on the front steps of the office building wearing the same outfit he wore the day we met: a black hoodie atop his work slacks. I saw the now familiar sideways grin. His eyes. I felt the uncertainty of taking the walk across the street to meet him under the street light.

We could beat it together. Our parents. His ex. I could help him. He already helped me. *Love is unconditional and accepting and brave.* I wanted a different outcome and I needed to change myself in order to get it. This wasn't about who was right or wrong. It was about giving more to someone than I had before. I fell asleep to the sound of him singing away his worries in the shower.

CUT

EIGHT INCHES OF my hair covered the salon floor. I stared through each blonde strand at the checkerboard tile, feeling my neck grow lighter with every snip.

Mike already ripped out more of my hair than what laid in front of me, but I kept searching the mirror – staring at my pale skin and desperate eyes – telling myself this was a decision I would've made even if he hadn't. The emptiness, my hollowness, numbed all logic.

I was cutting off my hair because the love of my life said he would pull it out of my head if I didn't.

Disagreements, moments of fleeting clarity always ended with him grabbing my hair at the nape of my neck, pulling me to the floor or slamming me against the wall. Things had gotten worse since I took him back, yet I knew we just hit a low and would get back on track. As my stylist snipped at each strand, I was sure this was our lowest.

Eight years earlier, a hair company approached me to model in a regional hair show. Expert stylists gave step-by-step instructions to new cosmetologists who scribbled notes and snapped pictures with their flip phones, waiting for new certifications.

Afterward, the makeup artists bronzed my cheekbones and layered on pale glosses before putting me in front of a photographer. The cut was stacked high across the back of my neck and layered fringe hugged my cheekbones, sweeping long bangs across my forehead. Trendy, and if lucky, my haircut would end up in one of those high-end hair magazines.

It was a cool gig for an eighteen-year-old high school graduate. The show brought applause and I enjoyed the attention. While my cut never made it into a magazine, and I only participated in two shows before MSU's fall semester began, I still liked the story.

That was the last time I had hair this short, a stark contrast to this moment where I was desperate to find solutions to problems I was trying to survive. Giving away my hair meant giving away pride, but it was a small sacrifice to make in order to find peace at home again.

Snip.

Another wisp of hair fell to the ground and woke me from my reminiscence. My new secrets, hiding in broken places, allowed me to feel. So what if it was only sadness and regret? It was still something.

I wished I'd never emailed the painfully sick man who lit up my computer screen with his thoughtful advertisements. Mike's words on a lonely night in December made me feel irresistible when I thought I knew how unhappiness felt.

Snip.

I wanted to be that girl again, but I wanted to bring Mike back with me, to put my head on his strong chest, and to dream while lying on him. I wanted to save him from the terror he was causing both of us. And I wanted that depression back. I wanted the simplicity and ache of it, a reminder I was alive and feeling.

I sat and watched my hair continue its slow sweeping fall, blanketing the floor in flecks of yellow gold. This wasn't happiness. This wasn't living.

How can I possibly sacrifice so much for someone who does so little? I couldn't imagine loving anyone the way I loved him in his brokenness. I endured pain to see him smile. I knew it would end too, if I could just hold on a little longer. Nobody could possibly be so full of hate for long.

The school year started just weeks before, and I thought back to the power and control I had in my classroom. I wouldn't have believed I would miss teaching, miss my kids, the way I did as I sat in that chair, but the last few weeks of demands from my boyfriend, who was also my boss, reminded me this wasn't a problem the year before. I only had to fight myself on color choices for the living room then.

Now, the constant belittling from Mike, who seemed to be irritated by my breath, and the girl who looked back at me in the mirror was broken. She wasn't me though, the haircut was a power play: a way to combat his eager hands. Unable to grab my hair, I thought maybe he'd stop.

Mike took Ann to court for refusing visitation, and she came out of it with a slapped hand and a fifty-fifty time split. He continued the battle after that day, pushing for full custody of his daughter, and the court appearances added more fragility to our time. The kids visits between our arguments gave me weekends of reprieve, but I was fucking tired. Exhausted. Undone.

To endure this. To fight that. It was too much.

And too much to give up on: the relationship, the income and the kids.

Having already sacrificed what I had, could it get worse? Not if I could get him to take his medicine.

As I saw the last bits of my hair fall to the floor, I realized I never felt heavier.

"Do you want me to style it for you, 'Fina?"

The stylist's words shook me and I stared at my reflection in the mirror. She smiled and put a hand on each shoulder, squeezing to confirm she was waiting for a response.

"No," I said, "you've done enough."

AN OPPORTUNITY

I FOUND A full-time ghostwriting job posting on Craigslist, for books, articles, and web content. Anything the client needs, it said. I evaluated the job description and pay. It claimed the books to be academic, biographies, fiction, how-to, non-fiction, novels, and technical manuals. Although I didn't think I could write all genres, I knew I could write some of what they needed.

I wasn't bothered by working with Mike, though it caused him stress and he ignored me at the office. I loved looking through the doorway and seeing him hard at work behind his expensive mahogany desk. He wasn't as noticeably eager to spend time with me outside of work after seeing me all day, and my job performance didn't make him happy either.

"I think I just expected more production, 'Fina. I'm not sure what to tell you, but my dad isn't happy either." He wanted me to do more. I wanted to do more too, but not for him.

I knew finding another job was critical in mending our relationship and my bank account. He didn't promise the position would last forever, and I didn't want to ruin us by staying too long. Plus his dad had to like me. Otherwise, I wouldn't be bringing in any money at all. The best I could do was to continue searching for a job while he paid me the little he could.

After sending my resume to the contact on Craigslist, I received an email asking me to interview the following Wednesday. This was the best chance I had at making one of my dreams come true: an actual writing position.

The day of my interview came and I skipped out of Mike's office. We needed a break from one another and I needed to prove to myself and to him I could earn my own income. Funny how a few months changes everything. I taught three months before, yet he seemed to have forgotten I was changing careers. It wasn't fair for him to expect so much from me so early, yet his disappointment lived in me, reminding me I had to make it.

I pulled out my favorite teaching outfit, something I hadn't anticipated wearing for an interview, and swept my bangs back with a bobby pin before heading out the door.

* * *

The company was in North County, the area where I grew up. Lucky for me, I knew where to find the building and how long it took to get there. I found myself there forty-five minutes early, parking on the opposite side of the building so no one saw me, and waited for an appropriate amount of time to pass before entering the suite.

Phil, a middle-aged man, and Courtney who was probably no older than me, interviewed me first.

"So you have an English degree, eh? That's great," Phil said, forgetting to make eye contact while he inspected my resume.

"I do. I graduated in 2006 and worked in a high school until now. You could say I retired early." I tried to find confidence in my answers, but I was nervous. If Mike didn't think I was good enough for his company, would a real writing job be too much? My eyelid flicked with anxiety as they shot off a few more typical questions.

"What's your biggest weakness, Sarafina?"

I couldn't tell them the truth, that I gave too much for almost nothing in return. Instead, I thought back to previous interviews and went with the easiest answer.

"I'm a bit of a perfectionist. In most cases, this is an asset, but I'm hard on myself when things aren't up to my standard."

It wasn't a lie, necessarily, and in many ways this mimicked a pattern in my current relationship: the questioning, always wondering who actually created the problem and how my reactions perpetuated his responses. Why was my home life following me into an interview? Unsure of how to answer my own questions, I tried to focus on the two people seated across from me. Their final question threw me.

"Have you always wanted to be a writer?"

Thinking of the year before when I thought I wanted to be a teacher, nervous now, a small bead of sweat formed on my upper lip. My lungs felt tight, my breath laboring quietly as I thought of the embarrassment this could cause. Masking the action by scratching my nose, I wiped away the sweat, thinking of an appropriate response. I didn't know how I could tell them I hadn't always wanted to be a writer, so I did what I'd been doing for the last several months while people asked me about my relationship or my absence in their lives...I deflected.

"When I was six, I wanted to be a butterfly."

Phil and Courtney stared across the table at me, unsure of how to respond. I smiled, attempting to show them I had a sense of humor. Seconds later the silence was broken when they both started laughing.

"I'll tell you what," Phil said. "You need to write an informative book tonight, covering the real estate marketing trends in our area. This book will be for someone who wants to learn techniques for success— someone new to the field. If you can do it, bring it back to me tomorrow and we'll see what we have available for you."

I was shaking. *An entire book in one night? Fuck.*

"Is there a length requirement?"

"Just as long as it needs to be, Sarafina. See you tomorrow."

Before I could ask another question, Courtney and Phil stood up and left the room, locking themselves into another office space on the right side of the hall. I could hear them talking animatedly, as if they picked up right where they left off before my interview.

This was the moment I would be able to try my hand at writing. Even though I was scared, I also knew it was the only shot I had to prove myself to my interviewers and my boyfriend.

I stopped for caffeine on the way home. It was going to be a long night.

* * *

Mike introduced me to theories about marketing by Seth Godin and Gary Vaynerchuk. He watched me frantically put the e-book together and, instead of reminding me of my inadequacies, grabbed his laptop and worked alongside me, researching the real estate terms I might need to know, even calling a long-time friend who worked in the industry.

"Sometimes you make proud," he said, putting his hand on my thigh and pressing lightly. "You're pretty damn smart."

I smiled at him and kept working, appreciative of a soft moment in the midst of our recent chaos. He kissed my temple and nudged me with his left shoulder.

"C'mon gorgeous, let's get you this job."

The next day, I sent the fifty-page book to Phil before sunrise.

Then I worked in Mike's office writing print ads for the local paper. But I couldn't concentrate. I checked my email every five minutes, hoping Phil replied.

"Time for another coffee?" Mike brought me a fresh pot and filled my mug with caffeine. "You've been working your ass off since last night," he said, "Looks like somebody got back in their groove."

Mike had become the man I loved again, the one who supported me and encouraged my dreams. I tried to remember the last time he'd done anything nice for me, and stopped when I realized nit-picking his weaknesses wouldn't make them go away. Enjoying the softness of our conversations, I finished the company's newsletter and the city's write up with plenty of time for new projects in the afternoon.

Phil's assistant finally wrote back at lunchtime.

"After consideration of your interview and further review of your qualifications, our owner, bestselling author and publisher, Phil Buckner, would like to meet with you. Are you available for a second interview? Friday at 3:30 p.m.?"

I looked into Mike's office and pulled myself out of my chair. "Hey, babe, I got another interview." I went to his doorway and leaned on the doorway.

"That's great, 'Fina," he said, looking at his computer screen. I wished he'd look up at me and show me he cared, but whatever he stared at consumed him. Only giving him a few more seconds to respond, I turned to sit back at my desk and continue on new assignments.

Mike finally looked up to find me back at my desk. "Hey you, I'm sorry. Let's grab lunch to celebrate, okay? We can eat and run by the pharmacy. I'd like to grab my Klonopin."

This job and opportunity meant I could distance myself from Mike, and maybe that's all we really needed, especially if he was taking his meds. Maybe this time I could get out of his office, if what they promised turned out to be true. I could survive without his help and he'd be helping himself.

And, if that didn't work, I could buy myself the time to get everything in order, to build up my bank account and make a plan. Then, once everything was in place, I'd make him leave.

STD

"FINA, MY DICK'S been itching for days. Who're you fucking?"

Mike sat in his black leather chair at the office with his pants unzipped, showing me what looked like razor burn. Swollen red blemishes, some appearing to be full of puss, lined the area between his hips and groin.

I didn't cheat. After feeling the pain of infidelity in my previous relationship, I couldn't cheat. I promised myself I'd never cause anyone that type of gut-punching hurt. Sometimes I wondered if I wasn't so vulnerable from my previous breakup, would I have given myself to Mike so freely after the short time we spent together? That point's moot; I was Mike's now.

He liked hearing himself more than anyone else, so I let him unload hateful accusations, leaving thick, heavy unfairness across my back.

"Tell me if you're cheating on me," he said, pointing down at his lap. I swear the redness deepened as he got angrier.

Choking over my words, I tried being neutral, a calming influence. "I don't know what to say, Mike."

He didn't often accuse me of cheating or dishonesty. How could he? I didn't have enough time in the day between working at his office and as a ghostwriter, keeping him happy and trying not to live in a house as messy as our relationship.

Sometimes his accusations and insults were only meant to leave emotional scars, and this was one of those times. Though I was thankful his anger wouldn't land on my face, his manipulation would stick with me, make me feel weaker for longer than a bruise would remain visible.

Medication, I thought, was the only way to fix this. He needed help. Even though I wasn't an expert, anxiety and paranoia drowned him weeks ago, and never gave him a chance to surface. His left eye hadn't stopped twitching for days. He needed his Klonopin, and maybe I did too. Talking to him about his medicine was touchy at best. Mike lied to me about consistently taking it, and he was defensive, belligerent, insulted me like I was the reason he needed it. *I'm so fucking sick of you acting like you're better than me,* he said, *did my parents put you up to this?*

"I need you to call him. Call David. Tell him you have an STD. I can't sleep knowing you gave this to anyone else."

The irony hung thick. He wanted me to call the guy who cheated on me twelve months before with a girl who was cheating on her boyfriend. Yet I was the one being blamed, called a slut, forced to own a disease I didn't carry. I couldn't help but wonder if David's sexcapades lead to me having a disease I didn't know about. Something was wrong with Mike's dick, regardless of whether or not I was always safe. Condoms weren't optional.

Mike grabbed my cell phone and scrolled through the contacts, looking for David's number.

"Mike, this is ridiculous. I'm not calling him and telling him anything. You're the one who's itching." Exhaling the hate and hurt he caused, I turned away.

It was true. I had no symptoms. My last trip to the gynecologist, albeit awkward, proved it. Her voice and words looped as he continued accusing me. "Oh, you're going to be an easy patient," she said. "You have a nice, clean vagina." That appointment was six months before, and the only person I'd been with since was Mike. No calls from her and no symptoms from me. *Was he fucking someone else?*

"Listen, bitch. You're going to call and tell him you're a dirty slut who gave me an STD and warn him to go get checked. Because if you think I'll let you ruin the lives of other people too, you're fucking wrong." His fist clinched the phone as he shoved it in my face. The screen showed David's number ready to be dialed. All I needed to do was press the call button.

I smirked, the lines of my lips expanding as I pressed the green call button. If I was going to be embarrassed, at least this might make Lacey and David upset about their choices. Maybe it was karma's way of paying them back for their dishonesty. And while I realized how manipulative and cruel this was, Mike's treatment of me made it easy to forget the person I used to be: the one who only wanted to help people.

If you hurt me, I was more likely to want to hurt you.

It's why I regularly thought about killing Mike. How life would be easier if he no longer existed, even though I loved him and wanted to help him. Every time he hit me, every time he yelled at me, every time he took my money, my hope of fixing him died more. And so did my memory of the girl I was before him.

David didn't answer. I clicked on the speaker and turned the phone away from me, allowing Mike to listen as David's voicemail kicked on. He grabbed the phone from my hand and ended the call, snatching my hand and lifting me off the floor.

"This isn't over," he said. He handed the phone back and I tucked it into my back pocket. "When he calls you back, you're answering and telling him." Mike turned away from me, clutching the crown of his head between his intertwined fingers. "Let's go get a drink."

Hunching in his shadow, I squinted in disbelief. "You want me to go get a drink with you? After all this?"

"Yes, 'Fina. I do." He turned to look at me again. "Because even though I think you're fucking someone else, I still love you. You can sit here alone or you can come with me. Your choice." He started for the door before I had time to answer the questions screaming in my head. *Is this how he thinks you show love?*

* * *

I'd been drinking a lot lately. Whiskey mostly. My anxiety drowned in the bottom of a tumbler. Normalcy came when I was too drunk to know what normal was. When I was only able to focus on simple mechanics and blacked out to everything else – when alcohol was involved. I knew it was fucked up and disgusting. Unhealthy. But none of it mattered with a glass of Jim Beam in hand.

Mike bought me several shots once we got there, but only drank one. We sat at the bar next to an old, red phone booth taking shots and playing PhotoHunt. Mike and I laughed a lot, sharing stories with the bartender from our early months.

"She wouldn't let me kiss her," he said.

The bartender leaned against the rimmed bar top, laughing louder than necessary, earning her tips by patronizing us with her company. She was in her late thirties, with long black hair and a tight shirt that didn't hide an ounce of her cleavage. She laughed at our stories, especially the ones where Mike and I would end up dancing in the house together. It was something we used to do often, hooking my iPod up to wireless speakers, slow dancing softly or skipping through the halls when we'd hear something fun.

"'Fina, do you remember when we slept in the Taco Bell parking lot after that Cardinal's game?" He chuckled hard and deep, grabbing the bar to hold him up. "That guy came up to dance with you, so you took the hat off his head and wore it, dancing away from him and back toward me."

After the team won, we ran to the oyster bar to see Kim Massey perform, celebrating, and forgetting one of us would have to drive home. Instead of risking it or spending extra money on a hotel room, we curled into one another in the back seat of his Audi. The next morning, we pulled over to throw up before making it out of the lot. We laughed about it the whole way home. He was wearing the hat I took off the man on the tiny dance floor.

"It wasn't until we got home that we realized..." He paused to laugh, refocusing and sighing from the jolt of happiness tightening his side. "We realized, oh man...you'd lost a sandal."

We played and lived like kids in the early months of our relationship, and when things started to turn for us, these memories reminded me why I loved him then. *Maybe I still loved him.*

He leaned over to kiss me. "Come here, gorgeous," he said. A throwback to the same days we'd been discussing. "Give me a kiss." He leaned in fast, cocking his head while confidently staring at me. Expectation and happiness gleamed in his eyes: two things I hadn't seen paired for weeks.

I leaned into him, fully releasing my anger and unhappiness, pressing my lips harder against his to shift the energy out of my body and embrace the soft, wet moment we were having in the middle of a crowded room. My phone was sitting on the dark wood of the bar top when it started vibrating underneath my fingers. I pulled away from him, staring as the man I used to desire resurfaced from the depths of his usual darkness. David's name appeared on the screen. "You don't have to pick it up," Mike said, pulling me back toward him. The bartender turned away from us, dropping a dishrag into the bussing tub and walking to the other end of the bar where a second couple pawed at one another.

"Of course I do," I said.

This was the moment I'd be able to show him my devotion. Playing this game, with people who didn't really matter to me anymore, would make him proud to be with me. I thought we'd go home and fuck the way we used to, and I hoped my conversation with David would be the reason why. Mike hadn't mentioned the questionable rash since we got to the bar, but this call would be a reminder, and I didn't want to ignore it and risk answering questions or changing our dynamic. I knew how to play his game.

"Hello?"

I walked into the phone booth and shut the door, dropping down onto the wooden bench and hoping to drown out the bar music. Static came from his end. I knew the echo meant David had me on speaker phone. Mike swiveled around in his chair and watched me from the bar, signing "I love you" with his right hand.

"Mike wanted me to call you. Apparently he thinks I gave him an STD," I said, smiling in Mike's direction through the sliding glass door.

The crackling air was the only sound between us. "Did you hear what I said, David? Guess what I think actually happened?" Accusation thrown, I knew he'd respond.

"'Fina, are you okay? I don't even understand why you're calling me."

"It's about your little whore and you fucking her before you stopped fucking me. Have you guys been checked for STDs, David? Have you ever considered how your actions impact other people?" I tucked the phone between my shoulder and ear, while my arms flailed and banged against the booth walls. I spoke to him like Mike spoke to me, mimicking his anger and accusations and remembering the last time I asked David for help and he refused. I lived through enough guilt trips to know what would wound David the most. Finally feeling something that night, first love, now anger, I became more and more aggressive. Feeling my preferred drug.

"I'm worried about you. What the fuck is this even about?"

"Don't turn this around on me, asshole. I asked you a question. Have you been tested yet? Is your slut clean?"

His silence spoke to me more than any words could. I knew the answer before he ever spoke it. Even though I should have been even angrier, the fact that I felt pleasure because of his fear felt disgusting.

"Do you think you have an STD, 'Fina? If so, how do you know he didn't give it to you?" David articulated a question I hadn't thought to ask myself.

I didn't know.

He was sitting at the bar, the bartender presenting her boobs to him again, sliding a towel across the grained wood in front of him. Mike had been drinking, doing drugs, staying out for nights at a time and showing up when he needed to eat or shower. He was hanging out with people ten years younger. Even tonight, when we walked into the bar, girls were there who knew him and greeted him with their eyes and smiles. But it didn't matter now. If he was cheating on me, it wasn't as painful as his words. I didn't need another thing to worry about anyway.

"Listen, did you and your little slut get tested after you left me or did you not? Because if you haven't, I need to explain this to my boyfriend."

Mike twisted around in his chair and presented his empty glass to me, tossing the stirring straw from side to side. He turned back around without another gesture. I knew it meant he was done watching me scream in the corner.

"'Fina, please," he said. "Please think about who you're with. I'm worried about–"

"Fuck you, David. Fuck you and fuck your fake concern. Go get tested." I interrupted him before he could say it. How can he be concerned about someone he cheated on?

I hung up, adrenaline streaming through my heart. Mike looked pleased. I sat next to him, thinking he might not turn his back on me in bed that night. I grabbed my whiskey and Coke and drank it down quickly, asking the bartender for another just as I finished the first. Even though he was pleased with me, something was wrong. "Make it a double," Mike said.

I didn't feel as good about the conversation anymore. David had made a good point. I wasn't sure about the man I was with. Just hours before, Mike had been so cruel. I felt worthless. None of it made sense. Still, here we were, Mike pleased and touching me like it was the first time.

"Babe," I said, squeezing his fingers between mine, "if you thought

I had an STD, why didn't you just ask me to get tested? Why have me call him?"

To show my question was honest, only to better understand, I looked down at his lap.

He laughed. "Well, gorgeous, it's as simple as this: you've been feeling pretty good about yourself lately, thinking you're better than me because I'm at the bar all the time. I know you don't have an STD. I wanted to bring you down a few pegs, and show you how capable you are of being a bitch, too."

I stood up, releasing my hand from his, working up the courage to walk home by myself. My purse was hooked under the bar and I hit my head as I stood back up, stumbling a bit from the surprise.

"Oh, and I am not paying you for this month's rent," he said. "You don't deserve it and I'll need to go to the doctor to get this checked out."

The bartender walked back over just as I was leaving. "You're not staying, darlin'?" she called from behind the bar.

"Not tonight she's not. I told her it was time for her to get home."

CARNIVAL RIDES

MIKE DROVE TO Louisiana, MO, to pick up Savannah and Blake early in the morning. We were taking them to the street festival in old town that night. The floors were swept and mopped, the furniture dusted. I picked up the puzzle pieces off the floor, still a mess from their last visit, and sat on Savannah's bed. My fingers jumped from one yellow star to the next, skipping the baby blue spaced between them. I missed the kids.

Mike went to his hometown to see them instead of bringing them to my house. He said it was because we weren't getting along. He was right. Even though I missed them, especially Savannah, I knew they didn't need to see us argue. His weekends with the kids brought me peace, so I didn't complain when he left on Friday afternoon. My house used to be filled with their giggles and I was excited to welcome them back inside. This weekend was my opportunity to prove to Mike how much our relationship was improving. That would get him to bring them back more often.

We watched them set up the Ferris wheel and Tilt-a-Whirl next to the train tracks two nights before. Things were getting better. Ever since I cut off my hair, he couldn't pull me by it anymore. And I learned it was best to keep my thoughts to myself when I was upset, because I was only going to cause an argument if I spoke without thinking.

* * *

Freshly showered, I brushed out my hair. I heard Savannah throw open the door and scream for Watson from the other room. She loved him. Watson loved her, too. On the nights she stayed at the house, he always curled into a ball and slept between her legs. She wrestled around, finding ways to touch him, hitting her elbows and knees against the wall common to our rooms. They had the opportunity to tumble again tonight. I smiled for the first time in weeks and rounded the corner anxious to see the little blonde girl, unconcerned they made it back almost an hour early.

"'Fina," she shrieked. I met her in the middle of the living room. Her excitement made her forget we usually started our conversations in sign language. I scooped her into my arms and felt her tennis shoes bounce off my shins. The static in her hair clung to the back of my shirt but it didn't bother me. I didn't want to let her out of my arms.

There was a honk in the driveway and I pulled back the curtains to see Mike and his seven-year-old son, Blake, sitting in the car. Mike pointed his middle finger at me then sternly pointed down the street, indicating he was ready to head to the carnival. I pointed to my hair and shook my head from side-to-side, hoping he would realize I needed more time to get ready. At the least, I needed to dry my hair.

I knew he wouldn't be happy if I wasn't wearing makeup – he always told me how embarrassing I looked without it – and hoped he'd decide to wait to avoid an argument. From the window, I watched Mike look to Blake and tell him to jump out of the car. Blake's head dropped in disappointment. His feet dragged on the pavement as he walked toward the door. I opened the front door and stepped onto the porch to greet them.

"Hey, buddy. I'm almost ready. I promise I'll be fast, okay?"

Mike put his hand on Blake's back and ushered him through the door. Neither of them said anything as they walked past. I inhaled the world, doubtful this would blow over without me being reprimanded. As I turned to walk into the house, I saw Blake's chubby face staring at me from the entryway. I saw the anger in his eyes and then I felt the gust of wind push against my face. He slammed the door. I stood outside, waiting to hear Mike make Blake open it. All I heard was the pitter-patter of Blake's feet running toward the kids' bedroom.

Our day just began yet I knew it was already over. With my hand resting on the doorknob, I let the warmth soak into each finger. Moments like this were becoming more common, where I wanted to turn around and walk away from my own home because I felt safer outside.

"Did you get locked out, neighbor?" My neighbor must've been standing on his porch watching when Blake closed the door in my face.

He tried to look upbeat but uncertainty pulled his mouth to the side.

"No, I'm all right. The kids, you know." I stopped talking before it got more awkward and I stared at him, swinging my hand off the knob and then back on it, rocking myself from the balls of my feet to their heels.

He turned away without another word, avoiding another awkward conversation. This wasn't the first time he'd seen our arguing and I knew my neighbors were watching the house.

I appreciated the smallest things in moments like that. The heat of the metal knob. The little revelations were what I had left and all that made me feel alive. The big things were easier to dismantle now. Blake behaved just as his father had several times before: no consideration for anyone's feelings except his own. I could feel each finger twitch against the others as I turned the knob and forced myself to face the unhappiness.

Mike and the kids were playing and unpacking in the bedroom. Watson was hiding in his kennel again. The guilt of leaving him inside with Mike hit me and I found myself unconcerned with wasting a few more minutes to be certain he was unharmed. Watson lifted his head from the bottom of the crate and rested it on my hand, looking at me with glazed-over, deep, sad eyes. We had our pain in common.

I walked past the bedroom refusing to look inside and turned into the bathroom, grabbing my hairdryer without closing the door behind me. To add volume to my short hairstyle, I flipped my head over and began drying my hair upside down. One of the only things I liked about my cut was how fast it was to fix it. Nothing else in my life was like that. I pulled at the roots with my right hand, massaging my scalp to try to ease my building anxiety. Soon, as I ruffled through each strand, the dryer was no longer needed. I turned it off and flipped my head back over to find Mike standing inches from my face.

"Blake's disappointed now. You have five minutes to finish getting ready and you need to put on makeup, otherwise we'll leave you at home and you'll disappoint Savannah. I don't like seeing my kids upset."

"Your upset kid slammed the door in my face, Mike."

"You deserved it," he said, sucking out any heat the hair dryer produced.

* * *

Blake spilled his soda into my purse while we rode the roller coaster. It was an accident, but my phone fell victim and unless I threw it in a bag of rice, I was going to have to pay for a new phone I couldn't afford. Lucky for me, Savannah was ready to visit Watson again, so I got home without much resistance from the other two. They stayed behind to try a fried Twinkie.

I carried Savannah back to the house. She would've walked but I wouldn't let her. I needed to feel loved. She always loved me and she held her right hand at the nape of my neck, pushing her fingers through my stacked cut. I walked forward, only allowing myself to feel her presence.

We made it to the house quickly and I let Watson outside to go potty. He didn't want to get out of his kennel, scared to run into one of the men of the house. I set down Savannah and replaced her with Watson, holding him just as tight as I held her. He always loved me, too.

Savannah looked up at me and tugged at my side. Tears made her eyes shimmer.

"I went a little potty in my pants. Can you help me get new panties?"

She was so innocent, so scared to be wrong. I saw myself in her and I began crying.

"Of course I can help you, baby. I'll be right there."

I walked into the kitchen to find a paper towel and dry my face. She was standing in the doorway waiting for me to help her. Even though the accident upset her, it was nice to have someone want my help. I wondered if parents often felt this when they were sad: a strange desire to help someone else in order to fill their own needs. If so, I guess I understood why sad people had kids. Maybe it helped them fill voids they couldn't before. I cried harder.

"Why you crying, Sarafina?"

I picked her up, feeling her damp bottom on my forearm and took her to the bedroom where I sat down on the bed again. Her dresser was empty – except for a pair of pink leggings – and I frantically searched her bag for a clean pair of underwear, pushing aside a stuffed white kitten and miniature hairbrush. Mike didn't pack any. I heard

Savannah's breaths shorten, her shoulders heaving as she realized I couldn't find anything.

"It's okay, baby. I think I have some downstairs."

I threw her laundry in the machine and put her in the leggings while we waited. I couldn't call Mike to figure out where they were because my phone was dead, courtesy of the soda, so we walked the two blocks back to the carnival hoping to run into them. We maneuvered around street vendors and groups of teenagers, anticipated walking into her dad and brother every time we found a break in the crowd. We'd been looking for quite a while with no luck and I started to drag Savannah around behind me.

Then I realized I didn't put my phone in the rice. Her accident distracted me enough that I forgot the whole reason we went home. We crossed the train tracks and looked through the front window of his office space hoping to see the boys inside, but they weren't. I squinted in the direction of my house, but didn't see anyone outside there either.

With little hope of finding him in the growing crowd, I took Savannah back to the house again. Her clothes probably needed to go into the dryer soon, and even though I was fairly sure my phone was ruined, I wanted to try to fix it. Mike and Blake were playing soccer in the front yard when we got back. Savannah ran to them and jumped in the middle of the game. They were occupied, so I ran into the house to fix my phone. I found it in pieces scattered across the floor. I knew a slamming door was the least of my worries. More than that, I knew I was trapped in my own house.

CARNIVAL RIDES: PART II

"WHY'D YOU BRING her back here if you weren't going to fix your fucking phone?" I didn't hear him walk through the door. And I didn't know how to respond. "It was ruined anyway. Are you that stupid? You couldn't even pretend to fix your phone when you came home?"

With every question he stepped closer, finally leaning forward to hang over me, use his size to intimidate.

"First you ruin Blake's day because you're too stupid to be ready. Then you ruin your phone. And then you didn't get my daughter here in time and she had an accident. You really don't want me to bring them here anymore, do you?"

Having the kids around made Mike behave, and Savannah had become one of the best parts of my life. Her adoration showed me I was lovable. We laughed together, and when I helped her with anything, she was always thankful. His daughter gave me the love I wanted from her dad, the love he refused to provide.

"I told the kids to stay outside so we could talk, so you listen closely. Don't you fucking make a sound. Don't you let them hear this."

He put both hands on my shoulders and pushed me hard. I fell back, trying to put my hands behind me to soften the fall but I wasn't fast enough. The crown of my head crashed into the cabinet below the sink. I bounced off the back and curled my legs into my stomach, hoping to dissolve inside myself. He crouched down near me, grabbed the back of my neck – the same place his daughter touched softly – and pulled me forward. I could feel my heartbeat through my wrist.

"Get up."

He pulled me up by my neck, the same place he grabbed my hair, and pushed me back down again. I didn't cower or curl up this time. I was silent, fearful of what would happen if the kids heard me cry or plead. I didn't try to break my fall either, my wrist hurt too much. Plus I knew it was a waste of energy. He would quit when he felt I knew he was serious. Every ounce of power I had left needed to be reserved for when he stopped, so I could decide how to protect myself for the rest of the night. When he realized my body was relaxed more every time he threw me down, he stopped and walked out of the house.

His voice was kind in the sunshine. The kids were laughing. I crawled across my kitchen floor toward the living room doorway and found the pieces of my phone. I picked up a few, holding them in my hand as though I could mend the damage. I heard him laughing, telling the kids to give him a few more minutes and then they would get dinner. He told them I wasn't feeling well, so I wouldn't go this time.

He walked into the house and stomped his booted foot near my hand, crushing every piece of phone still on the ground.

"Get up."

My head slumped. I knew I had to do what he wanted. I was someone whose only purpose in life was to please others, to do whatever was asked. A dog. *Was trying to help him through this really worth all of the pain he was inflicting?* It occurred to me then, just as it had every other time he hit me, that if he loved me the same way I loved him, he must be dealing with something far worse. I could take it. Otherwise, this abuse was senseless. He wasn't a monster. He was just sick.

I stood up.

Mike walked into my bedroom, slid my mattress onto the floor, and picked up my box spring – over his head – before coming back into the hallway. He shot a look at me, then pushed the door open to the basement and threw it down the stairs. Following the noise into the basement, he kicked every board in the box spring with his heel, breaking it into splinters. I watched as the metal springs rolled across the unfinished floor.

"You don't deserve to sleep on a bed. I'm fucking up your frame next," he said, standing at the bottom of the stairs with pieces scattered. His fingers were curled into one another making each knuckle white.

Mike leaned over, looking at me standing at the top of the stairs, and pulled at the last step moving it side to side until it broke free from the flooring. He ripped my stairs out of the ground, lifted them up to his waist and slammed them back to the floor. The wood cracked. My heart pounded. Everything I witnessed was unimaginable.

He started up the stairs, showing no fear as he came up the staircase he just ripped from the foundation. I ran to the bathroom, gripped the inside of the door and slammed it shut, sliding my body down the wall and digging my feet into anything to give me leverage. I was going to protect myself, but he never tried to get in.

Instead, I heard him walk back into my bedroom and thrash around. Back in the hallway, I heard him throw something else down the stairs. I didn't move. I hardly breathed. I sat there frozen through all of the noise. The sound of his footsteps finally led outside. I sat still until I heard his engine fire up in my driveway.

I crept out of the bathroom and crawled through the rooms, the tiny shards of my phone pricking my hands as I moved, until I reached a window. He was gone, or at least his car was. I locked the doors and stood up to see what all the noise was before he left. My bed frame and mattress lay at the bottom of the basement stairs, each piece of the metal frame bent and twisted on the floor.

But none of that was as significant as the conversation I had with the police officer.

* * *

I didn't have a phone or any idea when Mike would return with the kids, if at all. I never expected to see him act that crazy. Yes, he pulled my hair, tripped and pushed me. He said awful things. But I never imagined he would ruin my property, our bed, because of anger.

I was scared. If he came back and I was unable to make phone calls, I had no way to protect myself. Finally, I decided to walk to the gas station two blocks east of my house. This time it was over.

Pitch dark outside, the streetlights led the way through my neighborhood. The temperature was cooling off, which didn't matter to me. The jacket I wore hung off my right shoulder. I could hear the sounds of the carnival: kids laughing, horns honking on rickety rides and vendors screaming. We were the only ones to have our night end in a police report. I was sure of it.

I came to the gas station every morning before heading to work, but the attendants looked at me as though this was the first time they saw me. I walked into the gas station, trembling as I wiped tears from my swollen face. They let me use the phone to call the police. I allowed myself a minute to feel sorry for myself. Standing in the same place, looking bloated, red, and confused, I gave the police my address and explained I was walking back from the gas station. A police officer was waiting outside when I returned.

"Good afternoon, ma'am. How can I help you?"

"I need him to never come back. I need–" My voice broke and I looked down the street at the carnival. "I need you to help me."

"Well, you'll have to calm down first," he said, standing with one hand on his stick and the other thumb tucked into his belt. He was thin, near forty, with dark hair. He motioned me toward the house, asking me to detail the events of the day. He stopped several times, looking around at various misplaced items. His eyes glazed over and his head cocked backward. I felt as though he was more interested in judging my house than hearing my words. He stepped on one of the pieces of my phone.

"He spiked it against the floor. I'm not sure, but when I left it on the counter it was in this bag. Then I walked back in, after he came home, and it was broken like this." I began to hyperventilate as I remembered our first encounter with the police. Had it been long enough that the previous encounter wouldn't show up on my permanent record? Was this how we would end our relationship?

"Ma'am, you need to calm down. You're not making any sense. When did you leave? I don't get it. Start at the beginning." He walked back into the living room and sat on the edge of my end table, presenting the couch to me with his arm. He took off his hat and put it on his knee, finally humanizing himself. "Okay, um–"

That was how it began, the first conversation when I admitted he was abusive.

"He was mad I wasn't ready on time. And there's a lot of story in between, but when I came home and found him here, he was livid. He put the kids in the car and came after me." I pulled at the sleeve of my shirt and showed the officer the red indents in my collarbone left by his fingers. "And so he stopped because I, because, because I stopped fighting him." Deep sobs came between each statement. I stood up and ushered him into the hallway. "That's when he threw my stuff down there." The officer saw my mangled bed frame and began descending the stairs.

Remembering he'd pulled them from their foundation I panicked.

"Stop, you can't. You can't go down. He pulled the stairs up. They're going to fall in."

The officer turned to look at me and pointed backward. "Stay calm," he said. "They seem pretty sturdy to me." He walked down the stairs carefully, tapping his foot on each step before putting his full weight on any of them. The officer made it to the bottom of the staircase and looked around the floor at the broken bed frame. "He obviously didn't tell us about this."

That's when it became clear why he wasn't interested in anything I said.

"Ma'am, listen, he called us before you did. He said you went crazy in front of the kids. He said you're supposed to be taking medication and you're not. Is this true?"

Of course he called the cops. Why hadn't I realized? This was the second time. The first ended in his arrest. I was hoping this call would too. But the questions the officer posed were accusatory. It appeared Mike was better at this than me. I wondered if I was the first woman he treated this way, if he'd called the cops before on someone else. *Was this how he protected himself from getting in trouble?* I crumbled to the floor, unable to speak through my weeping.

I was trying to get help, to free myself from him, and the officer didn't want to hear what I was saying. Mike already convinced them of his innocence. I looked like a psychotic, possessive, lonely girl who was just dumped by her boyfriend. He looked like the dad who saved his kids from me. Nothing I could do would change this guy's mind, so I surrendered to my emotions and ignored him.

"Ma'am," he said.

"Just go away. You don't believe me and I don't need to be told I'm wrong by anyone else. If you're here to make me feel even worse, you're doing your job. Otherwise, there's nothing left to say." I pulled my knees into my chest and dropped my forehead to them. I watched tears drop onto my thighs and soak into my jeans.

"Ma'am?"

"Seriously. I can't beat him. He's manipulative and smart. He wins."

"Ma'am, please. He told me he was taking the kids to the mall, but I could hear boats in the background. Does he know anyone who might live near water? He was very calm."

We didn't know anyone in Lake St. Louis or along the riverfront. At least, I didn't. The police officer bent over and put his hand on the floor near my foot, looking directly at me as I lifted my head.

"It's just strange. He called first, then you. I was already on my way here because he called on you, so I thought you were calling to protect yourself. I see it now. Can you tell me everything again?"

He walked to his car and grabbed the necessary papers for me to file a police report. I showed him the hallway and the bathroom again. I showed him the twisted bed frame and broken box spring at the bottom of the stairs.

"There's nothing wrong with your stairs," he said, looking up at me from the basement, "but someone did a number on your bed."

I cried more, explaining I couldn't sleep there that night. I hadn't thought about where I would stay and didn't have a phone to make any calls. I certainly couldn't stay there in case Mike came back. The officer brought my mattress back up. He slid it into the bedroom and left it on the floor without a frame or box spring. "I need you to detail every second. Maybe even detail the things you don't want to talk about."

I couldn't write yet. I couldn't wrap my brain around everything that happened.

"I'm going to call him back. We told him we would. I need to see where he is so I can tell you if he's planning to come back here."

I sat on the couch with the paperwork in my lap. My palms were sweaty and the pen slipped through my fingers as I began writing. One paragraph in, the police officer stood over me, reading the words I scribbled onto the sheet. He asked me to stop and start over. It wasn't detailed enough, he said. I never thought words would be so hard for me. Writing was always something I was good at, but not in that moment.

I didn't know how to explain I wanted to make him better, that every time he hurt me I knew I could fix it, that my love for him was unconditional and nobody could protect me from him but me. That I wasn't perfect and thought it was probably my fault sometimes, even though I wasn't sure if I thought that because of him or me. How many times can you hear something before you believe it's true? I knew this was the first step in my recovery, and I needed every word I scribed onto the paper to be perfect.

"Do you want to press charges, 'Fina?"

The police officer looked to me as though I was telling the truth.

"He didn't pick up."

I asked him what it would do, how it would affect the kids, and if I could protect myself without pressing charges. He told me he couldn't be certain any of those things would happen, but my best chance at keeping myself safe was to go forward with the charges. So I did.

I packed Watson's kennel full of his food and bowls, a blanket. Then, I packed extra clothes and toiletries for me. The officer gave me a business card with his contact information circled and told me to call him the next day for a follow-up. He was going to call Mike, too. Watson and I pulled out of the driveway as the cop sat in his car, waiting for me to leave. He followed me to the highway and then turned around and headed back to the station.

Interstate 70 was full of cars passing me as I drove in the right lane, twenty miles an hour under the limit. My breaths still long and inconsistent, my chest was tight. All of this felt so unnecessary. If he only knew how much I wanted to fix him, he wouldn't treat me the way he did. I must not have done a good enough job showing him.

I stayed with my friends, Topher and Val, that night. I didn't talk much, just enough to tell them I needed to stay because Mike and I were fighting. They didn't ask questions, but their faces told me they didn't need to. Topher gave me a flip phone to use until I could buy another.

"I don't have much income, Topher," I said, thinking about my minuscule income as a ghostwriter. "I appreciate your help, but I don't know when I can pay you back."

"It really doesn't matter, 'Fina, just keep it until you're done. You're good for it. I know that."

This was the end for me. I knew it wouldn't get better if I stayed. Now that Mike rode off with the kids, it gave me a chance to focus on my own career and get myself happy again. I needed to be blind to our past. In order to do that, I needed him gone, out of my house, and out of my life. This was my chance.

AFTER THE COP CALL

THE NEXT DAY, the charges disappeared without explanation. The police had no record of any report or call, and I couldn't press charges if my police report was missing. Although I looked for answers, calling the police department several times that day, the officer who came to the house never returned my calls and the rest of them said they couldn't find any record of my complaint. I knew I was fucked.

I crept around the corners in my house and looked over my shoulder at open spaces. The drive to Home Depot to buy new locks prompted me to look through the rearview mirror more than the windshield. I didn't shower because I feared he would break in while I was naked and alone.

This was the day I was going to give up.

He controlled more than just me. *How the fuck did he get to the cops?* His power and reach terrified me.

Topher made me promise I wouldn't go back to Mike.

"Just don't do it, 'Fina. You've seen what he's capable of."

Going back wasn't an option. I would lose what little I had left, and I had to admit my failure, how ill-equipped I was to mend him. I had to stop trying. I was dead inside with nothing left to give.

"I'll follow you home tomorrow and we'll change the locks. He's gone. This is over," Topher said.

"I'll email his dad once you leave," I said. "If he isn't helping him with the charges, he'll keep Mike away from me."

* * *

Hi.

This isn't the first time you've received an email from me regarding my relationship with Mike. I'm sorry things are complicated.

We had another argument. He was upset about a few things and he pushed me down twice before ruining my bed frame.

After he left I called the police and the officer who came to the house advised me to press charges. Mike is being charged with third degree assault in O'Fallon. I filed these charges in hopes he would leave me alone for good. After the last cop call, he talked his way back in and it can't happen again. Our relationship is toxic for me, an addiction.

I care very much for your son and never intended for our relationship to turn into what it has, whatever that might be. My problem was believing I could 'fix' him. I anticipate he told you about the other day at my house (or at least about the dissolved relationship). I imagine most of what he told you is a lie.

I know you know he's a liar. And I don't think he's taking his medicine at all. He's manipulative and aggressive. I wish I saw this earlier.

If you can assure me Mike will not come with you, and he will not contact me directly, I will drop the charges. As I said before, I care about him very much and do not want to hurt him. I just want to move forward. I cannot do that if he tries to contact me. I know these charges could be extremely detrimental to his relationship with his children, and I would hate to be a part of the reason they do not get to spend time together.

I feel terrible I'm putting this responsibility on your plate. I do, however, know he will listen to you (and usually only you). He knows his livelihood rests in your hands. I feel if you tell him to leave me alone, he will finally let me move forward.

If his things are not moved from my home within a month, I will be taking them to Goodwill. I can no longer keep them here. I just can't. I'm certain that without these stipulations, he will randomly come back. That scares me. Please let me know your decision.

I dry heaved over the bathroom sink for an hour after I sent the email. Topher was gone, my locks changed, and it was my last attempt at keeping Mike away. Hopeful his dad didn't help him get rid of the charges, I thought the email might be a shot at keeping myself safe. Maybe, if I was lucky, Rick wouldn't know the charges disappeared and he would continue to protect his son – to enable him – and come get his belongings. Then the rest wouldn't matter. Rick would never find out the charges I pressed disappeared and I would be free of Mike's shit. Still, it wasn't lost on me Mike was winning. He'd get everything back without facing the consequences of attacking me.

I sat alone in the house that night, staring at the amber paint covering the ugly wood paneling in the living room. Life had changed so much. I recounted endless nights when I bandaged my fingers after scraping them on the floor staples, removing shag carpet remnants and blemishes, leaving behind traces of myself in the structure. Now it was hard to pay for it. Mortgage bills were overlooked. My income from the firm was gone and my ghostwriting income didn't match my outgoing bills.

I didn't manage it appropriately and I was about to lose the house. Watson nuzzled his head into my hand, as though he knew I was distracted. His cold nose left wet spots on my palm and I stared at them before closing my eyes and dropping my chin on his back.

I promised Topher I wouldn't go back again. Though I told lies to protect Mike while we were in our relationship, I couldn't do it again. I'd already given him his chances. But his belongings still sat in my house, and they haunted me on nights when I felt lonely. The kids' room was still set up, and his clothes were still there. It didn't matter to me that he was living without most of his belongings. But it mattered that I had to take care of them, even though I promised to focus on taking care of myself.

When his dad finally came to the house, I left to let him pick up his belongings without having to see me. I couldn't see Rick; he would remind me of his son. And, even though I was allowing him into vulnerable places, I knew he wouldn't mess with anything that wasn't his. The pain I felt was more about my choices, my failures, than it was about losing Mike. I knew he wasn't good for me, but I couldn't help but feel as though I could've saved him. That if I made different – better – choices, maybe I wouldn't be worried about what was happening in O'Fallon, in my kitchen, while I waited for Rick to leave. Maybe instead we'd be eating lunch on the floor or taking the kids to the park.

TWO MONTHS LATER

HE DISAPPEARED, vanished without trying to get back in. After two months, I finally felt safe on my own. It was getting warmer again in O'Fallon, the seasons changing with my feelings. I was alone, trying to make a living in the aftermath of our relationship.

Still ghostwriting, the job wasn't as busy as they'd told me it would be, and when President Obama was inaugurated clients succumbed to fears: they weren't going to pay to have a book written if it wouldn't sell. Driving from O'Fallon to North County was costing me almost as much as I was making, but I did it anyway, unable to give up on my dream. A strip mall was just built down the road and a new restaurant was opening. I applied for a position there, hopeful to earn extra cash at night while I worked at the writing office during the day. Lucky for me, they hired me at my initial interview, and I could work as many nights a week as I wanted once they opened their doors.

Two jobs would bring in more money, but they would also bring in more distraction. And the restaurant would open just at the end of winter. "That asshole is gone," friends said. And they were right. He was. But I loved that asshole, no matter how much I tried to deny it. Feelings don't die when we realize we've made a mistake, even if we want them to. They stick, haunting places we want to heal. How could I explain the breakup still hurt? How could I explain the complicated juxtaposition of emotions: I *was* happy he was gone, but I wasn't?

His memory echoed through my hallways into every room, his faint laughter and lopsided smile ricocheting off the walls and falling to the windowsills, absorbed by thick layers of settled dust.

The breakup should've changed me but the aftermath felt just as painful – I suffered alone. Savannah and Blake stole my dreams and I missed them no matter how hard I tried to ignore it. Ghostwriting and serving tables helped, but I wasn't making enough to repay my overdue mortgage payments.

I sold my couch on Craigslist. And my living room table set. I hosted a garage sale, selling household items in hopes of miraculously making enough to fend off foreclosure. Watching buyers load my belongings was aloe on a burn. Their hands full of my memories and nightmares, smiling as they threw pieces of me into their trunks. My past died a little with every sale, but getting rid of everything reminded me of my failure. It was red ink scrawled from a teacher, disappointed glances from parents.

The money I made kept my water running and my car in the driveway. It wasn't enough.

Losing Mike and everything else struck me as hard as he once did.

* * *

I was at work when he called. I took a drink order from a chubby couple and felt the vibration of my phone against my right thigh. The man looked over toward my leg, furrowing his wavy brow, and I smiled at him through the side of my mouth.

"Sorry about that," I said, sure my tip would suffer because of it. But he was kind and snapped back to the conversation once I acknowledged the distraction. I scribbled their choices onto the order sheet and said, "Be right back," before rushing away to see who called.

When I saw his number my throat walls clamped on one another, compressing hard until the veins in my neck were visible. I forced myself to inhale through my nose and gripped the bar railing with one hand while I sucked in the alcohol fumes puddled beneath me in the mat. The air burned like a shot of whiskey, and pooled in my stomach, unsettled bile and leftovers. *Why?* Trying to ignore the nausea rising in my belly, I let go of the railing and grabbed at the lid of the ice machine. I thrust my hand inside, glancing back at my table, hopeful they hadn't seen me panic. I watched them closely as I shoveled ice cubes onto the scoop. When I went to fill the cups, I missed. Distraction weakened my service, an unusual error for me. Cubes spilled onto the floor, shattering on the wood and shooting away from my feet, some sticking between the black rubber holes in the mat. I swore as the bartender passed me.

"You all right, 'Fina?"

I smiled as I blew the air out through my nose, wishing I could destroy my phone – and problems – as fluidly as the ice that'd just fallen. My cell phone vibrated twice as I picked up the scoop again.

This time it was a text, but I didn't read it. I had to work.

On the second try, the ice cubes hit and bounced off one another, clinking against the red, plastic cup. With each second, the tremors grew. I grabbed for the soda gun and my arm muscles liquefied. I knocked over the cup I already filled. The ice spilled out and onto the floor again, sliding under the beer cooler. I watched in disbelief. This wasn't happening today.

"'Fina? Seriously?" The bartender crept underneath me and tugged at my apron. "Get them their drinks and take a break, girl. You're losing your shit." I looked back up to see the couple at my table watching me. The man's wavy eyebrow was back. The woman knew I was spooked, her hand clutching her husband's lap. She tried to silently communicate something was wrong. "I'll be right there, guys. Sometimes these cups are slippery," I said, staring out across the otherwise empty floor. I whispered my thanks to the bartender, turning away from the table so they couldn't see.

I smelled like the fry cooks in the back, damp and breaded, and his call made it worse. Like something I couldn't scrape off.

After taking their food order, I rushed outside to read Mike's text. *What the fuck could he possibly want from me?* The backdoor led to an asphalted parking lot full of dumpsters. I leaned against the restaurant's brick wall for support, pushing my right foot into the structure. It was a feeble attempt at grounding myself, a last shot at putting back together what I'd lost inside. My hand fumbled for the phone, grabbing fear and regret, but I knew I needed to read it so I could get back inside and finish my shift.

"'Fina, I have cancer. Call me."

* * *

"Is it bad I feel relieved he might die?" I said to the bartender. Tears streamed down my chest and pooled in my cleavage, my work tank top dry and tight.

"You can go, you know. I'll cover your table."

The couple was still there, cat-like, nosey while they picked apart French fries and watched me fall apart behind the bar.

"But where am I gonna go?"

If he really had cancer, it didn't change anything. Or maybe it did. Maybe he realized the mistakes he made. Either way, I wouldn't know unless I called him back. And I certainly couldn't assume he'd changed or hadn't. Assuming got me into trouble. Guilt hung around the conversation like locals did the bar. *How could I possibly ignore him if he was really sick?*

My other grandma died of lung cancer my junior year of college. I watched her body eat itself from the inside out. She wasn't a health nut necessarily, but she drank apple cider vinegar and walked every day. When we were little, she'd grab us by the hand and hold us up while running around the store. "Come on, 'Fina," she'd say, laughing as I tripped over myself. Doctors explained one of the reasons we die from cancer is our inability to consume enough calories. Our bodies think we're starving and eat themselves, shutting down organs along the way. A dumbed down version for families of terminal cancer patients, I'm sure. But it always stuck with me as I watched her die slowly, how different the pace was when she was sick.

I was at the Incubus concert with my sister Bella when she finally passed. Sam bought me a meet-and-greet ticket for Christmas that year. A fan girl of Brandon Boyd, I had a countdown on my calendar until July finally arrived. On the night of the concert Sam acted cool until it was time to meet the band. Once we reached the table to receive our autographs, she looked straight at Brandon

Boyd, my mysterious, tattooed crush, and said, "I like your hat." That was it. Like "I like your music" or "I like your face" wouldn't have been better. She looked back at me after it slipped out, her golden complexion flushed out to the paleness of mine. After, between songs, I looked at her as I caught my breath, laughing, and teasing. "I like your hat," I said. It wasn't until after the curtain call that she read the text from my dad, *Hey, hon. Call straight to granny's after the concert.* We rushed to the house, making it before the coroner put her frail, gray body in a black bag. Looking back, I wasn't sure if seeing her in the hospital bed parked in her living room, mouth wide open, was the best way to remember her.

Mike's text made me see her again and I couldn't help but think of Savannah watching her dad die. I saw him lying there, skin draped over his bones like a blanket, while the bag was zipped shut over his head.

And that little girl, the only constant source of happiness in our relationship, watching death wheeled out on a stretcher.

"I don't believe you, Mike." It was all I could think to write at first. Opening lines of communication was more than I wanted to give. Still, his confession concerned me.

Just months before we broke up, he made me cup his balls and feel a bump between them. "Does this look or feel funny to you?" he asked. But he laughed as he did it so I didn't think he was serious. "No, 'Fina, really. I got tested a few months before we met. Doc said it wasn't problematic yet."

"Yet? Jesus, Mike. Why am I just now hearing about this?" I asked, frustrated he kept such important information from me.

"I think it's growing," he said, vulnerable for the first time in months. So I felt around on his scrotum, humbling both of us to the fact that nobody was ever truly safe from sickness. Sure enough, there was a lump. I'd asked him to get it checked out before we split up, but he'd become erratic and defensive again, so a doctor's visit wasn't a top priority.

I told his dad about it once, asking him to encourage his son to go see the doctor. Rick was the only one able to reason with Mike, but he was also the only one who could dangle a paycheck over his head. So it was easy to assume his text was true, that his dad finally forced him to have it checked out.

"'Fina, please. I know you hate me and I don't blame you, but I'm on my way to get an ultrasound and I have Savannah. My mom couldn't watch her and I can't bring her with me."

"Why do you have her right now? Where's Ann?"

"Court proceedings are finished. The judge granted me full custody. She lives here now, full-time." His response, the finality of the dreaded court proceedings, brought a lighter air to the conversation. At least one of us had good news.

It wasn't Savannah's fault her dad hurt me and left me in ruins. I couldn't ignore how helpless she was in all of this, and I knew exactly what he wanted.

"I'm at work. There's a kid's play center in the same strip. If you want to drop her off to me there, I'll stay with her until you're done, but that's it. That's all I have for you."

"We'll be there in forty-five minutes."

I called the owners of the bar and explained what happened. They let me clock out and said I could come back after, if I was feeling up to it. Regardless of the drama, I still had bills. The realization of life continuing when I wanted it to stop, to smash a vase into the wall and watch each glass shard fall to the ground. To walk through it barefoot and bleed out all of it. If only I could solve the pain by inflicting more. That's all I wanted. And I was about to do it by letting her and him back in.

* * *

She was wearing a skirt and boot pairing I bought her for her third birthday six months before. Mike picked her up out of her car seat and put her down on the pavement outside of the play place. Her pink suede boots hit shallow puddles in the parking lot as she screamed, "'Fiiiinaah,'" and ran toward me, unconcerned with looking both ways before meeting me on the other side. I ran toward her to be sure she didn't run in front of cars and scooped her into my arms. She put her tiny hand on the back of my neck. Realizing she hadn't seen me in months, she put her head on my chest and said, "I love you."

"We're both excited to see you, 'Fina," Mike said, interrupting our moment.

I swayed my hips, turning Savannah away from the conversation. "Stop it, Mike. What time will you be back?" I turned away from him then, avoiding eye contact and putting her back between us. Savannah squeezed my neck, looked up at me like I wasn't real, and then put her head back down to feel me. Her ear was cold against my collarbone.

"I'm not sure. I'll text you again once it's over. I don't know exactly what I'm in for today. I could need to talk to a specialist about surgery."

"Well, we'll be here. Keep me posted."

I walked away from him without looking back. It was hard enough to be near him, knowing the power and control he had. All I'd wanted was to love him, without worrying he would change again. That's what happened when he was around. No matter how cruel or dangerous he was, looking into his eyes and seeing him smile always showed me his softer, vulnerable side. I wanted nothing more than to help him again. To show him what an amazing person he could be, if he would only let people in.

I couldn't think about it any longer. I put Savannah down once we reached the sidewalk. She ran to the door, pulling hard at it and smiling at me. He honked as I reached her. Savannah waved, and I turned around to see his taillights pulling out of the parking lot.

My eyes watered as we walked into the smell of bleach and pizza. Savannah ran straight to a purple tunnel and crawled inside. She was so excited she forgot to take off her boots and I heard her little feet squeak as she made her way to the other side. I took her jacket and my purse to a table, paid for tokens and found her tumbling down a tube slide, giggling loudly. I grabbed her out, pulled at her boots and handed her the gold coins.

We went from game to game, hitting gophers with soft mallets and grabbing candy with metal claws until we had more prize tickets than tokens. She purchased a tiny pink ring that matched her outfit and stuck Pixy Stix in her skirt pockets, fearful she would lose them before I let her open one. Her final prize, zoo animal stickers, came in different colors and shapes. She kept putting the stickers on my forearms and giggling. I left each of them exactly where she stuck them to my skin.

Two hours after arriving, we left and went to my work for some food. Just as we were about to order a cheeseburger plate to split, Mike texted.

"Hey, gorgeous. Where are you guys? I see your car but you're not inside."

I wanted to tell him we would meet him after lunch, but he knew we were close. It was pointless to try, even though I had no intention of hanging out with him that day. It would be too hard. I loved him regardless of how things ended.

They didn't start that way, after all. Once I loved someone, even someone undeserving, I couldn't just stop. I knew my feelings would fade with time, but enough time hadn't passed. With the news of his sickness, every soft feeling for him I ever had surfaced. I could only ignore it for so long before everything blew up in my face. I told him we were sitting down for lunch and he could either find something to do or join us. He responded before we could order.

"I'll buy."

* * *

They left after lunch. Savannah hugged me tight and Mike pulled her from my arms. She didn't want to go, she said. He thanked me, attempted to hug me before I pushed him away, and took her home to Louisiana. I went back to work, busying myself with everything that didn't involve him. But he was in every conversation I had with guests. Maybe they had icy blue eyes or blonde hair. A deep, penetrating voice. Confidence.

A week later, he had another appointment. We hadn't talked since he left after the first one, but he wanted to pay me to watch her again. I refused the money and offered to babysit at the house. He brought dinner back with him and told Savannah they were leaving after they ate. Mike got everything ready, and when I walked by the living room, I saw the food on the floor. Mike noticed I was questioning this. He looked up at me from the floor.

"For old time's sake," he said. It reminded me of the night he moved in, when we promised to make this a tradition.

Two weeks later, he brought her back again for his follow-up appointment. "Want to go to Jimmy John's for dinner?"

I agreed to go. I wasn't ready to leave Savannah again, unsure of when I'd see her next. If ever.

I ordered a beach club and a plain turkey slim for Savannah, then picked her up off the floor and headed to the soda fountain. Two girls sat in a booth near the back, showing their texts to one another and giggling as they gossiped. One looked up from over her phone screen as I took Savannah to get her Sprite. "Your daughter's beautiful," she said. The other girl turned to look at us over her shoulder. "Oh, she looks just like her momma."

Mike walked up to us just as the second girl finished. He put one hand on Savannah's back and another on my shoulder, dropping his head between hers and mine. "Thank you," he said, "I have two gorgeous girls."

I smiled at them before turning to Mike and silencing him by handing him Savannah. I filled our drink cups and sat back down.

"Cut the shit, okay? You know this isn't easy for me."

"I'm sorry, Fi. It's just that, well, this will say it better than me." He pulled an envelope out of his jacket pocket and placed it in front of me. I tore the sealed flap open and pulled out a piece of paper.

This time he wrote me a letter.

Hello, gorgeous.

Consider this the wakeup call I needed. It's not easy to admit your faults, especially when they're as big as mine. The truth? I'm not perfect. Nobody is. But my eyes are open again and I know what I lost.

A smart, beautiful woman who loves my kids as her own.

You're going to be a great mom someday, and I hope I get to be a part of it. I know. I know. How, right? After pushing you away and forgetting what's most important, how can you trust me?

It's simple, blondie. I'll prove it. In therapy. With or without you, maybe both. Whatever you want, I'll do. That's a promise.

Life is too short to ignore what makes you happiest, 'Fina. And you are that for me. We deserve more than we ever gave each other, and I'm ready to heal the hurt and make you happy again.

"This isn't fair," I said, setting the letter down on the table and tearing open my sandwich wrapper.

"C'mon, 'Fina." He pointed at the table of girls we'd just talked to. "Could the timing have been any more perfect? It's another sign, right? Just like all of the other ones with us."

* * *

Every appointment, sometimes twice a week, I watched Savannah while he received the treatments he wouldn't tell me about. And then, a month after our first visit, he had two appointments on two consecutive days. So he asked if Savannah could stay with me, on my mattress, and he would stay in the spare bedroom on her twin bed.

I didn't sleep well that night, and I listened to him clean up the mess he made in the basement that sat untouched, a constant reminder of the day I called the police. Before his second appointment, he left a business card on my table for the therapist he wanted to see – wanted me to see with him.

I called the therapist while he was at the doctor and set up our appointment for the following week. Working it out, that's all this was.

HAPPY BIRTHDAY

WE'D BEEN WORKING toward getting back together for two months, and he was coming to see me in O'Fallon as much as he could. Once a week we spent an hour with a relationship therapist who asked us to work on communicating. Mike believed our problems stemmed from me backing away from our problems, and I believed he had to work on managing his anger. We walked away from most sessions feeling like we were regaining momentum: he was back on his medication and I was communicating with him as best as I knew how, always opening up about how his previous attacks had killed my trust in him.

We went to dinner after counseling, him always footing the bill. And most weeks, he'd leave me with a bit of money to put toward what he owed me: a sign he knew I was struggling and wanted to help. Plus, after he told Rick we were working on our relationship, he offered to pay me to work for the company again. His doctor reconfirmed he didn't have cancer, sharing that Mike would need to continue getting tests done to figure out the cause of his growth, but that it wouldn't kill him. At least not yet. "It could become a problem at any point," he said. And we both knew he couldn't risk skipping appointments any longer.

Our relationship status was never discussed, though he called me his girlfriend in introductions and conversations with others. With things looking up for both of us, I felt safe in his arms again. Two months without an attack was a record we hadn't had since before the abuse began.

He was still going out at night without me sometimes and I was okay with it. Mostly, it was when I had to work at the restaurant. My one-year anniversary for leaving teaching was just around the corner. So was his birthday.

* * *

"Tomorrow's my birthday, though," he said, straightening a line of coke with his credit card. "It's not going to kill you."

"Mike, what's going on? Things have been so good," I said, unsure if I'd missed warning signs that his behavior was returning.

Three lines on his desk mocked my inexperience and fear. I didn't want to snort cocaine. I didn't want to smoke it or shoot it either. *How does this even work?* Once, after prom, my then-boyfriend's older brother put some on his lower lip and I refused to stay at the hotel, fucking livid he would invite us to his drug den.

Getting drunk was one thing. But cocaine? This was the first time since then I found myself in a room with it. I shook uncontrollably. Mike didn't care. He didn't want anything to do with my excuses.

I didn't want anything to do with his drugs, but I knew his mood. It was back again, in full force like I hadn't seen since we split up the first time. *It might be better for me to do what he asked than to take another attack.*

I stared down at his desk, at the thin lines of white powder, and remembered the night before we met. How the snow on the ground reflected the light from the stars so perfectly. How the train brought with it so many wonderful nights. But not now. Now I had to choose a nose full of blow or blood. *I fucking hate that train.* The man who wanted to work things out was gone and I was staring at a monster again.

He set a rolled up twenty on the desk. It stopped itself on my pinky and specks of powder fell back onto the brown wood. He'd already snorted his portion. I breathed through my mouth, terrified to take in anything in front of me.

"It's not going to snort itself." He squeezed my shoulder, pushing it down and directing me onto my knees in front of the mess. "If you don't want to make me happy, you can go home now and I'll deal with you after I get there. Don't waste my time," he said, holding onto the crown of my head, pushing me closer and closer to the cocaine.

My breath was slow enough to leave the drugs undisturbed. I closed my eyes and held in the tears.

Sniff.

I pulled my head back and he squeezed my nostrils shut as I looked up at him standing over me. "Suck it in." He smirked wildly as I snorted his victory into my system. Proud and amused, high and pain-free. He let go and I felt the cool air fill my packed nostril.

"Round two is ready. You did good, baby."

My throat throbbed and tightened. "I don't need more. I already feel it," I said, hopeful one line would satisfy him.

"But I did three, 'Fina, and I want you to feel as good as I do." He pushed my head back toward the second line, the soft remnants from the first stuck to my fingerprints. "We were really working toward making it official again. I really want you to do this." And I knew he wanted me to pledge myself to him by doing coke. A twisted request from someone even sicker.

Two was more than enough. The shaking subsided. The drugs were working their way through my system. This was two more lines of coke than I'd ever done. Two more lines than I ever wanted to do. Panic and anxiety filled my chest while the numbness in my throat grew stronger. *Was I suffocating?*

Mike pulled my head back again, holding strong to the back of my neck, and pointed down at my face.

I stood up, brushing the coke onto my jeans and walked toward the door. "I think I'm just going to go home, Mike." He was going to hang out with the local guys at the bar, the gentlemen who sold him this shit. I was twenty-seven years old with snot and white powder dripping from my right nostril.

He leapt over the side of his desk and grabbed me by the back of the neck, pushing me back toward his desk, pressing harder with every step. With one hand on me, and another firmly pointing toward the drugs I left, he screamed, "I put this here for you. I paid for this because I thought you'd like it. Don't make me feel like you're wasting my money."

We rounded the side of his desk and he threw both hands on the back of my head.

He wasn't laughing anymore. I hung limply in his grip, submitting. *It was easier this way.* The more I resisted, the harder he'd push me. If I wanted to get out of the night with only having to snort one more line, I needed to surrender.

"Bend your fucking knees, 'Fina. Get on the ground."

I was eye level with the drugs and I couldn't feel my throat anymore. I couldn't feel anything, except the tingling behind my eye socket and the dry heat in my chest. Just months before, I was a teacher. Someone students looked up to. And now life was a dirty, dishonest mess. I was ashamed and weak. Brainwashed.

"You're going to snort this present I got for you, or I'm going to slam your fucking head into this table. And if I have to, and you bleed, you'll ruin the mahogany, you little cunt." *Sniff.*

"Good girl, 'Fina. I love it when you listen to me."

I sat there again, watching silent tears fall onto the once coke-lined desk, afraid of him and what I'd allowed myself to become: an addict's girlfriend, a user, and a voiceless woman.

"Take off your pants."   I cried on the floor, feeling for the button of my jeans. "Jesus Christ, 'Fina. Do I have to do everything?"

He flipped me over and pulled at my clothes, pushing aside my underwear and taking me from behind. I looked out the front window of his office down to my street. The porch light was all I could see, but I knew it was there. I knew Watson was there, hiding somewhere so he could sleep. I thought about my neighbors as Mike pushed himself inside me, how different our relationships were since Mike moved in. And I let him finish on my back just as the final train stopped in town for the night.

"I might not be home tonight. The guys and I are going to stay at the bar after it closes. You're going to like how you feel. Lock the office after you clean this." He walked toward the door without looking back.

I walked home after waiting for him to leave, my pants pulled around my waist with the button undone. I didn't care anymore. My throat was throbbing. My tears were gone. I needed to figure out another way to leave. I was going to do it this time, if I could come up with a plan.

So I wrote myself a few notes. I sat at the kitchen table with tremors shooting through my body, scribbling down the names of people I could turn to when I left him. Topher and Val. Maybe Ellen.

I hid my list downstairs, underneath the dryer in the back room of the unfinished basement. Every step calculated, even when I was fucked up. Then the paranoia started. Every clank from the old pipes or creek of the doors caused my eyes to twitch then jump, then stare toward the room where the sound originated. I carried a butcher knife through the house, swinging it around every time I heard anything.

I lay in the bed wide-awake, hoping he wouldn't come home until the next day.

He did. Thirty years old and flailing like a child. His parents were taking us to see *Les Miserables* at the Fox Theatre, a surprise. Neither of us had slept.

"I did too much, 'Fina." His voice trailed off. "My body is fucking shaking."

I stood in the hallway, watching him level the house like a tornado, searching for an outfit respectable enough for a trip downtown.

"Come on, baby, I feel like I'm about to have a heart attack. Please help me." He stopped and stood in the hallway inches from me, pressing his lips into my forehead. I felt his body tremors through his mouth.

"I need a shower. Please help me. Come on, 'Fina, you can't be mad at me on my birthday." He hugged me then, tight and comforting, the exact opposite of how he shoved himself into me the night before. He pulled me into the bathroom, caressing each invisible wound.

"I'm so sorry, 'Fina. I'm so awful at all of this. Last night was selfish and stupid, and I'm too old to be doing that crap anymore. We've come so far and I ruined it."

Mike stood under the water, pale and shaking, while I sat in my tiny bathroom watching him try to clean his freckled back. The humidity was heavy and filled my lungs with vapor, a relief from the dryness caused by the coke the night before. In a rare moment of weakness, he was gentle and kind. His voice was soft but his eyes spoke louder, a forgiveness rested behind them haunting our conversation, begging me to help and forgive him. And I knew that feeling would be gone once he felt better.

This is what safety feels like.

Sitting on the bathroom floor, damp from the shower mist, I dreamed of the days I wouldn't worry about him throwing me to the hallway floor. I knew I'd get there eventually. Celebrating the small reprieve his drug-induced sickness provided, I thought about my hidden list. A moment to rebuild strength, that's what this gave me. I needed to escape.

"Do you have a towel out there for me? You're awful quiet, baby."

As I handed him his laundered towel, I dreamt of the possibilities of the night before. I wished he would've snorted one more line and killed himself.

It's just for us.

Better behavior followed the cocaine and him raping me. It seemed I couldn't get rid of him, even though he lived apart from me in Louisiana. A month passed since his last attack and it was now June. He always showed up at my restaurant and sat at the bar while I worked. The bartenders and owner were charmed by him with the same cocky banter he used to charm me. Their comments didn't make leaving easier. Neither did his presence. *How do you leave someone who won't leave you alone?* The guilt I felt for using drugs outweighed logic.

Maybe I was in this because I deserved it. Or maybe I was trapped.

Embarrassed by it all, I refused to talk about that night with the therapist so, in his eyes, we were still moving forward in our healing.

Depressed and living a lie, I hadn't told my friends much about his involvement in my life. I didn't understand it, so I didn't expect them to either.

* * *

"But, baby, you know I shouldn't drive up to see you until tomorrow."

My MacBook leaned against the mattress. I was naked under the covers, ready to fall asleep when Mike texted me, "Skype." I worked at the restaurant that night and he had late meetings. Too lazy to shower after a slow shift, I stripped off the scent of fried pickles and peel-and-eat shrimp before throwing myself on top of my bed. Sex was the last thing I was thinking about.

New to both of us, Skype made us feel like we were together on the nights when he was working in Louisiana and I was in O'Fallon. Savannah started using it to talk to her mom when she was with Mike. He wanted to play with it too, but only when the kids were asleep.

"Mike, I'm really not feeling it," I said, flipping the covers off and setting the computer on top of them, lying lower than the camera to get a flattering angle against the curve of my ass. I flicked my feet from side to side, awkwardly moving like a child to avoid a serious conversation.

"Come on, 'Fina, it won't take long."

I sat up on my elbows, my nipples grazing the comforter. "It's just, this isn't a great idea."

"Who'll ever know? It's just for us." He smiled and tilted his head to the side, something he probably felt looked playful, asking me to do yet another thing I didn't want to.

Once, when I told him I didn't want to drive down and see him, he jumped in his car and showed up at my work unannounced, staking one of the tables in my section for the rest of my shift. He fucked up my table count and tip money. I told the therapist about it in a session.

"'Fina, he has a fear of abandonment, just like you. Can you see why staying with you all the time is something he wants? Surely you can understand that." The therapist's words insulted me and validated Mike. When we left, he warned me never to tell him no again. I knew exactly what he meant and I had no intention of making my life harder than it already was. I chose not to tell the therapist this, too.

Being naked on Skype with him, doing the things he was asking me to do, well, it was just too much for me. "Baby, please don't ask me to do this. I'll make it up to you tomorrow night when I'm with you, I promise."

"I won't ask again, 'Fina. Don't make me show up there."

I knew he would. Even if I left, he'd find me. He'd drive around town or sit at the office and wait for my Bug to pull down the street. He'd punish me the next time he saw me, use thick words or the back of his hand to hurt me. My own discomfort with my naked body wasn't reason enough not to submit. I sat up in front of the camera, my torso completely bare, rolling my eyes and nervously tucking my hair behind my right ear.

"You have the best tits. Now, go get the vibrator and show me how you like it."

My hair fell across my forehead and tickled my nose as I reached across the bed and into the top drawer of my dresser. The velveteen bag brushed against the grain of the wood. Just beyond the pull strings was where I left my bullet, a tiny vibrator he bought me when I told him I'd never used one. "A girl your age should know what she likes," he said, brandishing the bullet. On one of our first nights with it, he lit my gut on fire.

I opened myself to him in ways I never experienced with someone my own age, and he took full advantage of my eagerness, teaching me how to be a lover.

"This is what sex should be like," he would say, and, in ecstasy I'd beg him to stop, laughing all the while. "I like making you cum, baby."

I'd used it on myself before, but never while he watched. Now he wanted me to use it with my laptop propped between my thighs, the full shot, while he jacked off at home.

I was inexperienced in all-things-masturbation and unsure how to start. My previous attempts at self-pleasure usually ended up with me in the shower or just giving up. I never used a vibrator by myself.

"Put it on your clit to start. Once we get a good angle, I'll direct you further."

Bare-chested, he leaned against the chair and thrust his hips toward the screen. Mike was ready for the show.

I turned on the vibrator and let it pulsate between my fingertips, rolling the head through my hand. "Are you sure I have to do this?" I hoped he'd change his mind when he saw me hesitate, but he was silent. When I looked up I saw he already started. "Dammit, 'Fina, if I finish before you start, you're going to owe me. Come on."

I rested on the bed and kept my knees shut, hopeful he'd see plenty.

"Not good enough, baby, I need to see it all." His words were short and breathy, already affected by the show. Although I didn't want to do this, hearing him turned on helped me ease into it a little. Plus, my computer was already as close as my last OBGYN, so I had no reason to pretend I was modest.

The hum of the tool against me sent flickers of warmth through my stomach, but I stared off at the wall hoping to avoid him seeing my face. My physical engagement didn't mean I had to like this. He was forcing me to show myself masturbating, and I never felt so much like an object, so heartless and unheard, unseen for who I was. I raped myself of my own dignity.

I tightened my eyes around the burning behind them. Closing off the air flow might keep me from crying, so I fought it back while giving him the show he wanted.

"Turn around and put it inside you. I want to see you fuck it." I froze there hoping he'd forget what he asked. "Fucking do it, 'Fina."

On all fours, I put the vibrator between my legs and pushed it inside me as I bounced back and forth, crying heavy tears and gasping for air with my head shoved into the comforter. He finished while I was on my knees. I stayed motionless while he moaned and unloaded.

"I'm going to reward you for this," he said. "The next time I see you, I'll eat your pussy, baby, just like I used to."

I was nauseous at the thought, hot regret and disgust filling my throat.

"And guess what? I taped the whole thing so I'll always have it."

"Wait. What? You did what?"

"I taped it."

"That's not possible," I said, unsure if it was.

"Look, it's all here."

And it was. My legs wide open, my vagina and the vibrator. He taped the entire thing.

"Now I'll always have this to remember you."

If there was ever a reason to try to make it work between us, video footage of me masturbating was the best one.

BLACKENED

LOUISIANA, MIKE'S HOMETOWN, sits on the Mississippi just south of Hannibal, Missouri, the boyhood home of Mark Twain. People travel from across the country to glimpse at the majestic setting of Twain's best works. The natives, at least the people I met while living with Mike, spent more time in the woods – or in Louisiana – than the tourist town. Avoiding visitors became a priority, so the small-town life, reeking of alcohol and country folk, outweighed the nostalgia in Hannibal.

When Mike's dad asked him to return to Louisiana for office support, Mike couldn't say no. The O'Fallon location hadn't been as successful as they'd hoped, pulling in finance business from only a handful of insignificant companies. Rick needed to track Mike's work or his home life would, once again, get messy: Mike's mom wasn't wasteful and she hated that her husband let their son spend company money on every trend and program he could find. Mike's parents often argued about this, one of the ongoing conflicts in their relationship, and the family knew they'd talked of a divorce because of it.

Mike always longed for approval from his dad, who provided him an income that was triple mine, even without a college degree. Opposites, he hated his mother. Her resentment grew taller than the reeds mulched into her landscape. Having spent her working days as a high school history teacher, she valued higher education and belittled her son's success, believing he didn't deserve what his father earned. Even then, even loving him, I knew she was partially right. He was a silver-spoon baby turned adult. Things were handed to him without Mike ever having to struggle or work.

"She hates me," he'd say. Weekly family dinners fueled the growing rift, and we left an hour before anyone else because Mike couldn't resist the urge to rant at his mother. Like clockwork, he'd carry on with, "I'm going to buy the business from my dad and run it someday," on the way home. In both instances I believed him.

His mom wasn't nice to him, always insulting his parenting ability or talking shit about him, even to me. Sometimes trying to convince me I should make room for his ex-wife, that she should be invited to family dinners and holidays. I washed after-meal dishes with her enough to know she wished they'd work it out. Still, as peculiar and selfish as her demands were, she encouraged his ex to try to get back with him even after she knew what he did to women. She knew he was dangerous, having picked up the pieces of his broken marriage, but she never warned me.

I met Elizabeth, his mom, shopping at the Mills Mall in North County. Holding Savannah's hand at the Starbuck's counter, cold – apathy unlike any I'd seen – she stared down the mall's east wing, looking through passersby as if they were as empty as her.

"I sure hope you have good birth control," she said.

Most of her concern was directed at her bank account, in case my uterus swelled with Mike's third kid. I knew she'd never compliment him, and I think she was part of the reason I made so many excuses for him. If he was bad, why did she still insist on being around him?

If he was that bad, why didn't she just fucking tell me?

She was rich and spoiled and forgot what it was like to be without. She convinced me money made good people narcissistic, this bon mot coming from a woman who used to share the same passion for teaching. Compassion dwindled to nothing in the years since leaving her classroom.

Mike's parents succeeded in several ventures and they owned and rented a couple houses in and around town. Once they earned enough to live on one salary, Elizabeth left her teaching job to stay home. Loaning Mike the house on Sunset rent-free didn't matter to them, except it fed his mother's contempt. Furious about coddling him still, she didn't flinch about the money.

The distance between us bred ugliness and insecurity. Mike drove to O'Fallon, a two-hour drive each way, to visit, and spent less time in the office than his dad hoped. So when Rick finally told Mike he'd start charging him rent and would take the car off the company policy, Mike stopped showing up at my work as often.

His departure insured oxymoronic days for me: freedom tasted sweeter than the blood he drew. Still, I loved the man he was when we met: talented, determined, and passionate. His arms warmed me on cold nights. Now he wanted me to make up for the lunch breaks when he couldn't get away.

"After everything I've done for you, 'Fina, don't you think you can drive up here two nights a week?"

Every shift. Every night. He was with me or I was with him. The only thing worse than the travel was choosing to stay home. The guilt. Sometimes, though, the night's silence soothed my brokenness enough to face him again. I'd stay home instead of making the drive; his anger grew, exposed me to danger.

To keep Mike happy, Rick offered me a position writing public relations pieces for the *Herald* and *Courier*. Press releases, advertisements, and newsletters, day in and day out. But it would have to be from Louisiana, he said, saying he needed me closer to the media.

Accepting the job meant I could afford to stop waiting tables. It meant I could pay Magnolia's mortgage, even though I wouldn't be living there. I could start writing for myself, working toward earning my own money, even if I had to move away from everything I loved.

* * *

I spent hours on the red couch at the house on Sunset, writing about finance, staring through the front windows down the street into the high school. I didn't have to sit in the office every day, but I did have to be in town in case one of the papers needed me to bring anything to them – Rick's stipulations on my employment.

Friday night lights peeked in through the curtains in the fall and the marching band sweated through summer practices, blaring instrumental renditions of the "Cupid Shuffle." Most of the time, I enjoyed the work, and Watson always sat with me, the only other living creature who endured every second of the dysfunction between Mike and me.

He curled his head around my thigh, reminding me I was loved, as Mike's gravity bong mocked me from the kitchen. The foggy glass barrel looked on from the other room, reminding me of his deception. It hadn't been long since, "I promise, 'Fina. It's just for the occasional stress release." I decided it was time to confront him when the bong became a counter-top fixture. His moods were stable for a while after I moved in. On the upswing again, him and me and our love and his betterment. We'd get it right someday.

Nobody fell in love to be ruined.

He smoked and drank himself oblivious and made sure I knew the reasons. "Quit being so fucking judgmental Miss I-Left-The-Classroom-Because-I'm-So-Talented. Just because you think you're better than drugs, doesn't mean everyone else has to feel the same, you self-righteous bitch."

I felt better because he wasn't hitting me. But his verbal abuse had become more painful than any time he left a bruise.

When the screaming became too much, I shut the world off. We hadn't been to therapy since we moved to his hometown of Louisiana. I disconnected my voice and heart and head. His abuse increased in frequency and became less formulaic. Random irrelevant comments set him off and I felt it easier to remain silent than deal with one of his lectures. Mike was throwing away my anti-anxiety medication, claiming I didn't need to take it, and becoming more and more vocal about how unnecessary it was as time passed.

"That shit doesn't help you, 'Fina."

I knew I was suffering when I started smoking weed, too. I hated his usage and I certainly couldn't believe I was smoking, but I became number and number to daily activity. I didn't want to get dressed or eat, sometimes starving myself for a day. Since Mike was making me use my income to pay for groceries, I wouldn't eat so I could save money to pay my mortgage. Still, there weren't enough jobs to keep me afloat. It's hard to value anything when you're worthless. If my anxiety prescription bothered him, I could go without it. One of us could have his needs met.

I imagined him when the house was in order: always pleasant, his left dimple manifesting as the water sloshed around the last dirty dish. My jeans were warm to the touch as a pizza baked. If I could mop the floor before he got home, it would ensure a good night. His deep satisfaction surfaced in my daydream, rounding the corner and swaggering into the kitchen.

"When you're proud of this house," he would say, "I'm proud of you." I'd loosen my grip on the counter and meet him in the center of the vinyl floor. He'd place his chin on the crown of my head. His breath would kiss my temples and neck. I needed a moment like this soon to remind me why I stayed when our love was all wrong. It had been weeks. The front door opened. "Where are you, 'Fina?" he asked.

I only got out, "In here, Mi–" before he met me in the kitchen. No dimple in sight.

"Can you fucking believe my father? He's not paying my car payment. Says it's not a company expense," he said. And I knew tonight wouldn't be good to talk to him about his bad habits.

"Oh, Mike, I'm so sorry," I said, and walked straight to the bong to move it out of the cleaned room. Hopeful a full belly would calm him, I pointed out the kitchen timer going off with my free hand. "The pizza's ready. Do you want to sit down and talk about it?"

He froze, anger pouring from him hotter than the oven. I put the bong back on the counter and, just in case he decided to hit me, I dropped my head and stepped to the middle of the floor, avoiding eye contact and cabinetry.

"Did you do anything today? Explain to me what it is you do daily. If we weren't paying you, my father wouldn't restrict my car payments," he said. "I really don't think you're owning up to your end of the deal here. I've never met anyone who can't multitask. You made a pizza twenty minutes ago, but you sat on your fat ass up until then, didn't you?"

Tears blurred my vision. But I couldn't cry. If I did, he would call me weak or tell me I was selfish. Past experience taught me he would say I wasn't listening to his concerns and only focusing on my own irrational feelings. I stood in the kitchen waiting for the inevitable. I would either cry or puke from the fear of crying. Tonight wouldn't end like I'd planned, and I'd get high again.

"I wish you supported me. I really wish you loved me like I love you. I don't know why I love you either," he said. His volume increased, the distance between us closing. Mike took a few steps toward me, reached out his hand and lifted my hanging head at the chin to force eye contact; he needed to witness a moment of submission to feel superior again.

"Do you know how much I love you, 'Fina?" I stared back at the monster in the kitchen. He was quiet and calm, a sharp difference from moments before when he burst into the room. "Do you? Here, let me show you something, blondie." He clutched my right wrist, pulling me across the room with him as he would a leashed dog following its owner.

From atop the refrigerator, he pulled down a zipped, purse-sized bag. I hadn't seen it before, but I knew exactly what it was. Each tooth of the zipper released itself with a *click*. Mike began smiling with his eyes closed, bag still in hand. I took a step backward, hoping again to miss the corner of the cabinet when he attacked me. His body swayed back and forth like a mother cradling her infant to sleep, slow and methodical. He pulled me in to his arms and continued rocking.

Behind me, I felt the bag fall from his hand and hit the floor. It was empty. "I love you so much I could kill you, baby," he said, a slow, crescendo laugh bubbling from his lips. It haunted me, looping in my head and echoing off cabinets. Dizzy, spinning between feeling the gun at my head and all of the other moments he'd hurt me. Unstable and flashing between the present and past, my life hung at his finger curled around the trigger.

The cold round barrel grazed my right temple. His hand shook and the gun swung between my right eye and ear. I dropped my head again, hoping my submission would stop his anger. He turned my head until our eyes met from the force of the barrel.

"It's your turn to speak now. I said I love you," he said.

Silence flashed between us. I tried remembering the last time he looked this happy. I was shaking and my thoughts disappeared. I begged him to stop, reaching out to his right arm, pleading for him to realize how much I loved him.

He swatted away every embrace.

The pizza blackened in the oven, the scent of burning crust fuming, causing the heavy tears I held back to push against my sinuses.

"All right, little girl. I'm tired of your games tonight. It's time for bed. Go get ready," he said, releasing me from his grip. He placed the gun back on top of the refrigerator and walked straight to the bedroom.

I went to the bathroom to brush my teeth and cleanse some part of me I could control, hoping to escape the awful realization that nights like this were normal.

SUNSET

AND THEN HE THREW me down the basement stairs, smashed my cell phone, and tried to choke the life out of me at the house on Sunset.

Shoot me or slit my wrist.
You've already taken my heart, my soul, my mind. I'm worthless.
These last few seconds aren't wanted anyway. This is what you've made me.

I'm going to die tonight. In an unfinished basement where you hide your stash, so the kids don't find it. You're such a good dad.

Comfort comes from the concrete that envelopes my body on all sides. I collide with it and, because I know what's to come, I feel life in the pain. What's more fucked up? That it feels good or that I know I'm only momentarily alive anyway?

Consciousness is fleeting. Luckily, I'm delusional. I thought you loved me.

Your warm hands that used to cup my jaw as you kissed my forehead are now suffocating my lungs. Let go, baby. Pick me up and tell me you didn't mean it. Cup my face again. Kiss me. Make those promises. I'll believe you.

I don't remember what life is like without you. And I don't think it's worth it if I have nothing left. You've become the only reason I want to live; your grip gets stronger and stronger around my neck...

At least you're touching me.

ONE HOUR AFTER

HIS DAD THREW OPEN the heavy door minutes before I was supposed to leave and rushed down the narrow hallway. Tears covered the floor in the master bedroom as I tried to grab every piece of myself. Anything left behind would remind Mike of the days and nights he made me his ragdoll. His distorted memories of me, of our life, would lead him back to my front door. Nothing could stay.

"'Fina, I'm calling Sprint. I have a spare phone. It's yours. Can you hear me? You can't drive back to St. Louis without it."

I pulled at the sweaty grip of my T-shirt, releasing it from my back hard and fast. The air was cool as it moved up my spine, the scrapes from my fall stinging and tightening. The pain reminded me of the drop from the first step to the bottom – how far he threw me in only a few seconds.

Rick handed me his old Palm phone, staring at his feet. Mike must've called him after throwing me down the stairs and smashing my phone on the concrete basement floor. When he left the house, bong and wallet in hand, he threw hatred and threats at the walls. "Two fucking hours, 'Fina." The door slammed behind him and I knew I was safe. I had two hours to get out before he returned. I ducked under each word and crawled into the bedroom, locking the door behind me.

"It's the best I can do right now. Don't worry about sending it back," he said. His deep wrinkles reached across his forehead like a warning.

I had no idea how long I had been staring at the wall.

He stood in the hall in his freshly starched trousers, determined to avoid looking at me or my naked breasts. I heaved and gasped, focusing only on counting to four with every inhale clutching my shirt tighter against my stomach, tears dripping onto my shirt. Rocking back and forth, counting, doing it again. My eyes were swelling shut and I knew I had to leave.

Mike was going to kill me.

But that didn't stop my desire to fix what went wrong. It became obvious to me Rick and I would have this conversation about his son again if I didn't leave right away. Our track record proved it.

I tried to stand for the first time, fearful the throbbing meant my left ankle was broken. My heart beat through my toes and with every passing second it and the swelling intensified, sluggishly filling them with enough pressure that they grew numb and hard to bend. I grabbed at the accent chair near the door and with slow, methodic movements, rested my upper body on the seat, attempting to alleviate the fullness in my foot while I put on my sopping T-shirt. Standing alone sent shock and drainage into my stomach, but my ankle didn't buckle. Thankful for one thing going right, the tears came back again.

"Let me take your bags to the car," Rick said, still looking at anything but me.

My fingers pressed into the walls of the hallway, leaving a trail of snot and blood to the living room then the front door. Every knuckle and nail bed a blood-soaked red turned white as I grasped the wall. I was so close to freedom, the pain didn't matter. Nothing mattered but the sunlight shining through the front door.

Outside, heavy branches swayed as though nothing changed. I wanted to watch them, to freeze time and forget about my past, my fear, my broken life. In a few moments, I would drive home to an abandoned, empty house.

A house just like me.

I lifted my foot off the patio enough to hobble down the three porch stairs and grip the black iron railing leading to the driveway. At the bottom of the path, my Volkswagen Beetle's trunk had been hoisted open. Mike's father stood next to it, watching me struggle toward him.

He handed me my keys.

"Thank you," I said. Now I was the one staring downward, unable to make eye contact.

"'Fina, promise me. Please. Promise me I'll never see you again," he said, standing tall in my tiny shadow.

My eyes burned with exhaustion and regret. My tear-soaked collar clung to my chest. Listening to this, to him, made it real. I wanted to throw up every toxin Mike left behind.

"You need to be with someone who takes care of you. You can't fix everyone, 'Fina. You can't fix him," he said. I grabbed my flip key from his soft, weathered hand and nodded.

"I'm serious. Please take care of yourself and find someone who wants to help take care of you. Nothing else matters," he said.

Carefully, I began to lower myself into the driver's seat, fumbling for balance, and sanity.

"If I ever see you again, I won't talk to you. You can't keep doing this to yourself. He's not good for you."

Surprised he had more to say, I stared into his sad eyes and wished his son broke up with me the same way.

I pressed myself into the leather front seat as he closed the trunk. The click of the lock solidified it: I was leaving for good this time.

"I just wanted to help him, Rick. I thought I could help." I looked up to find Rick walking away from the car, understanding and nodding. For the first time, I realized I wasn't the only girl he'd had this conversation with.

My hand trembled against the key in the ignition. I went through the motions, even though I wasn't ready.

Mike's dad was already up the stairs and inside the front door by the time I moved my car from reverse to drive. Nothing else I could say would matter and his words, "This is it for us," helped me back down the driveway.

The outline of his high school filled my rearview mirror, an unbreakable brick citadel where Mike once ruled. His new castle, a tiny ranch full of nightmares and lies was visible in my left window for the last time. This was his world, this place. And I hated it.

I put my car in drive and left, still reeling.

As I rounded the first turn toward Highway 61, a familiar black Audi sat on the shoulder of the road. Before I realized it was Mike, the phone his father gave me buzzed and I slowed down enough to look at the message.

"Is it too late to fix this? I love you, 'Fina."

Without stopping or replying, I listened to the world around me as I drove home. Dark bruises caressed my wrists and the blood on my knuckles hardened into tight scabs.

None of it mattered then. My worries were bigger than the injuries I knew would heal.

My house waited for me two hours down the highway. The local water and electric companies were searching for me across the state, but soon they wouldn't have to look far. If only I had the money to pay them.

I had twenty dollars in my pocket. I left the rest of my money in his house.

THE AFTERMATH

IN HER DREAMS, *life is filled with lavender-scented paper and silk blouses. The ground is always below her, so searching for gravity isn't necessary. Neither are all the self-affirmations or classes on self-esteem. She's a graduate of the school of healing and an active member of a society who returns good deeds.*

It's the opposite of her waking hours, when tears stream down because everything sounds like loneliness. Even busy streets. She can't commit to putting herself into an unsafe world to discover the truth of her desires: she wants to move forward, but fears her future: she's not a puzzle in her subconscious musings.

She's a woman who understands life only gets better when risks are taken. So she makes left turns when her gut says so. Even though she knows where the road straight ahead leads and enjoys the adventure in getting lost close to home. It's okay to learn new routes back to the most known places.

Her dreams are in color, and her real life seems safer when she lives in black and white. If she doesn't know him, he can't be trusted. If she knows him, he's already proven he's not good enough.

But in her dreams, everyone is good and decent and fair. More than that, every heart is given freely and equally, so the outpouring of love is prevalent. Nobody has to be scared to fall. Souls are crimson and amethyst and sapphire.

She stays awake knowing the longer she keeps her eyes open, the longer she'll be able to go back to the world inside her head and heart at night. She runs extra miles or works extra hours to become exhausted, numb. She's never refreshed because her mind works madly while she's covered in blankets. She always wants to go there because she's free of all of the insecurities of when she's awake.

She says she believes someday her dream world will become a reality. It's better to stay awake, but living in the grays and blacks and whites isn't always easy. It's hard to silence the redheaded sirens who take her crashing back into dreamland.

THREE HOURS AFTER SUNSET

MAGNOLIA WAS SILENT and dark from the outside. It was noon and almost 100 degrees. The mulch I laid with my grandma was strewn across the yard, dried through like fossils. The mums, once as golden as champagne, were dead. She would be disappointed.

My neighbor noticed as I pulled in the driveway and stood near his car waiting for me to get out. After arriving, I put my car in park and stared back, never moving from the driver's seat. He walked away, his belt holding up saggy pants. It didn't matter that he only wanted to greet me.

A large sign from the city beckoned me from the middle of my yard, indicating the long grass was intolerable, embarrassing, and ticket-worthy. I ripped it from the ground and dropped it on its side, trampling my showable sins on the way to the front door. I didn't need a neighborly hello or a public display of criticism, and I didn't give a fuck about two inches of scrutiny.

The clunk of every step punched through the hallway into the empty rooms. Two white, industrial-size trash bags held the remnants of my life: clothing, shoes, and writing papers. My computer. I dropped everything in the living room and fumbled down the hallway toward the bathroom. Watson, as traumatized as me, hung close to my heels, following through the mess.

Six months before I met Mike, my dad and I gutted everything here but the shower. I didn't know what a wax ring was then, but I replaced it, amazed by my ability to learn and develop my independence. The room felt strange now. The toilet seat was cold. And the girl who updated it, young and optimistic, wasn't the same one sitting in its unaffordable, overwhelming darkness.

Letting go of the wall and reaching behind me for the toilet handle, I cried for the first time since I made it home. Silent and exhausted, I pushed down hard, hoping the force would magically make the toilet flush even though I couldn't remember the last time I paid my water bill.

A lucky pull, it flushed on the first try, so I tried again knowing water might've been left from before the city shut off my service.

It flushed the second time, too.

I cried more, my gut breaking the silence and throwing out relief.

The faucet spit brown, filthy water into the sink, swirling and splashing toward the drain. I placed my hand in the freezing stream to interrupt the cycle. The water broke chunks of dried blood from between my fingers. It was an ugly shade of humiliation. When it finally cleared, I tossed handfuls of clean water at my swollen, splotchy face. For the second time that day, I counted to four while I took in air, trying to remember I was still alive.

The sun poured through the window, across the white shade and down to my feet. I reached for the light switch and flicked it up, pushing my luck for two miracles, then looked back down. The only light from the room was the same stream from outside.

Between back bills, late fees and reactivation costs, I owed the electric company $660.

I sat slowly, taking in every second. He hurt me. I left.

My house was haunted, my neighbors and town watching.

Maybe I was the ghost. Maybe I was just as dead as my flowers.

SURVIVING THE VENOM

NOBODY ACKNOWLEDGED HOW, instead of the venom, power had been sucked from my veins. I was weak. I allowed the abuse to continue. I suffocated beneath sheets of hatred and resentment. Breathing didn't seem worth it. The weight of guilt might collapse my lungs.

The nightmares continued. I tried to remind myself I was worth more than he allowed me to be. But everything except the physical abuse continued after I left. The blood, tears and bruises faded, but the desire to admit he was right – that I was useless – remained.

Friends tried to provide comfort, but the gap between us grew. They couldn't understand it was my fault. I backed away from those who didn't know me. And if they couldn't see something wrong, the flaws so evident to Mike, then they never saw me anyway. Alienation. Hearing I was worthless felt honest.

Friends who said I was recovering were clueless.

I was used to the broken pieces and the cold sweats after a night terror. I resented people who saw my beauty because it was fake. It had to be. Nothing I knew before the abuse was real.

Now, a month after I left him, colors deepened, became more vivid. Feelings remained raw. Pain felt good. I forged forward anyway, hoping to be rescued from the nightmare, knowing I was my only savior.

How could I be revived? I had no pulse, no heart, no core or gut left to tell me where to go. The only remnants were hatred and suffering. Tears and sadness and longing. I spent time recalling every moment I could've walked away, noting how stupid I was to stay. The warning signs...

I was the bitch who now wallowed in the foulness that only a whore like me could create. I hid myself behind makeup and I drank because that's what stupid women do.

And that's where society finds battered women. Hiding from life.

Cutting our legs while shaving to make sure we're still human, to be certain we still bleed.

* * *

Mike was everywhere and I frantically tried to hide, to find the safety of before we met. It was elusive. I knew I would never be safe again. He knew I was alone. He let me know he was around, working at the office just a block away. He mocked me.

Every chrome-detailed Audi that drove by was his. Every insurance agency advertised in his language. Every song was a remembrance of our moments. The way things changed, even the misery I felt, reminded me of living with him. *Wasn't I supposed to be happier now?*

"Baby, I miss you." I didn't have enough money to change my number, so he'd be able to find me until I could. His regular texts and emails reopened old wounds, and I inflicted more, beating my head against the dresser or ripping and scratching open skin until blood fell from my arms.

I didn't answer him. He alienated me from most of my friends and family. I was broke, broken and alone. Still, a tiny wick inside me asked to be lit. It kept me from going back. I sat alone in my bedroom, creating a list of the household items I could sell to try and save my house from foreclosure. I prayed somebody would rescue me from the terror, because I didn't feel like I knew how to save myself.

His face was on a billboard less than a mile from my home. He posted ads in the restaurant – my former part-time job – and his company's pens were in every gas station I went to for my morning coffee. Without talking, he found every way to reach me.

Initially, I thought I was being paranoid. So I checked other nearby gas stations to be certain I hadn't cracked. No pens. No advertisements in other restaurants. He was claiming my territory as his own. If I wasn't going to answer, he was going to force me to see him.

It was time to move. He would always manipulate me if I stayed. If I wanted to recover, I knew I couldn't do it where he could find me.

THREE DAYS AFTER SUNSET

I MET TOPHER junior high, although our friendship wouldn't start until much later. His dimples were as deep as mine, but the depth of his blue eyes garnered him more attention.

At the beginning of our seventh grade transition, students were required to attend a two-day introduction to the school and our classmates. He was one of the best looking twelve-year-olds in the building and, since old classmates were spread between new junior high teams, we knew who to keep an eye out for fast. Before classes started, my friends' notebooks were decorated with his first or last name and tiny hearts doodled around one or both.

I remember all of this, even though I wasn't as enamored with him as everyone else. I didn't like competing for attention, so I always found the semi-attractive best friend of the best looking guy and went for him. That's how I ended up dating Steve, my first boyfriend, for six years.

Topher was around as long as he was dating one of my friends. First Ellen, in eighth grade, who let him get to second base on the couch at my friend Jackie's house. Then my friend Megan, who claimed his virginity.

His family moved to St. Peters after two years of high school, so I didn't see him much before graduation, but the one who stuck around, and the reason for our connection, was my college roommate, Dani. They had an on and off again romance, induced by pent up emotions and Captain Morgan. After two years of weekend visits to Springfield, he decided to transfer schools and ended up being my classmate again.

He quickly bonded with my college boyfriend at the time, Chris, sharing playful sarcasm and love of beer.

"You two are perfect," he said, "I want a relationship like yours."

He spent a lot of time with us after that, inviting us to his parties and even hanging out when we were sober. So when my three-year relationship with Chris ended, he was there to pick up the pieces. That's when we became best friends.

I wasn't surprised he drove forty-five minutes across the county to change the locks on the house the night I left Mike. It didn't shock me when he paid my electric bill without asking where my money went. He was the first person to offer me help after I left Mike. To this day, I believe he and his wife, Val, would offer anything I needed.

Once the electricity was turned back on, I could stay home. I used my MacBook to locate an unsecure Internet connection and spend hours on my mattress, applying for minimum wage, part-time positions. I was broke and unemployed, ghostwriting jobs became scarce, ruined by the failing economy.

The horizon was lit in golds and ambers. The moon would be out soon. This time of day was always the scariest for me. I worried Mike would show up on my doorstep after work, like so many times before.

The dust on my black dresser grew thick. I sneezed and my eyes itched as I became more exhausted with every day that passed. The only way to avoid fear was to avoid daily chores and hygiene. I ignored anything that felt too difficult to handle, mostly everything.

* * *

It was three o'clock in the morning when I heard shuffling outside my house. Watson heard the sound first and ran to the front door, barking furious little warnings toward the yard.

I grabbed my phone, fumbling over the sheets three times before I reached it.

"Watson, get back here." His paws pattered down the hallway toward me, but once he heard another clank he sprinted past me and leapt onto the bed, trying to see what danger stood outside.

The footsteps were heavy, clunky, manly, and moving away from the front door. The chills I felt dissipated through my fingertips. How had he gotten to the front door without me knowing? My house had two other entrances: a locked storm cellar door to the basement and the mudroom door, with broken-out windows from when Mike stumbled into it and shattered the bottom pane. If whoever this was broke in through the kitchen, I would have more time and space to escape.

Adrenaline pumped pain-killing endorphins into my ankle and I knew I would run, even though it was still sore from the day I left Mike. Unable to pay for a doctor's visit, I assumed my ankle was only slightly bruised or sprained since I could walk on it a bit.

Then I heard the chains. Heavy ones in the driveway, rattling along the ground.

I rolled onto my stomach and pushed my body upward until I was on all fours. I dialed 911 without hitting send, holding the phone between my hand and the mattress as I crawled to the left side of the bed. From there, the streetlamp outside allowed a sliver of light through the window. It hit across the concrete driveway to the right of my Bug, a spotlight in the darkness of the night.

The chains came from a worn out red tow truck. A woman and a dog were inside the truck and the headlights shone onto the trunk of my car. The driver stood in my front lawn with a clipboard, marking something down as he stared toward my driveway.

My heart rate dropped as I pulled open the window shade. That man was trying to take my car.

I quickly threw my hair back and rushed to the front door, grabbing a white tank top from the floor. I held my phone in my hand, still ready to press send, angrily squeezing it like a stress ball.

I hadn't been outside in two days and it was significantly cooler. I crossed my arms across my chest and rested each hand on the opposite shoulder, to avoid the embarrassment of the driver noticing my hard nipples.

The woman riding in the passenger seat saw me on the porch and, without speaking, signaled to the man in my driveway. He turned to face me, his back to Mike's office. As I stepped out onto the sidewalk, I remembered how moments before I was worried Mike was trying to break in.

"Are you Sarafina Bianco?"

"Why do you need to know?" I asked.

"Is this your 2007 Yellow Volkswagen Beetle?" he asked. Again, I asked why.

"I'm here to repossess your car, ma'am. You're two months late on payment. I have the paperwork here, but I'll need you to sign it."

I stared back at him without speaking. Three days ago, the love of my life threw me down a flight of stairs and tried to kill me at the bottom. After nearly dying, after crying my eyes swollen and all but shut, I drove home to a house with no electricity.

The lights along the train track flickered behind him, as if to remind me of how all of this started. I wanted to run the two blocks to the train tracks and throw myself on them. "I can't give you my car," I said.

"Well, you don't really have a choice," he said. "I can give you ten minutes to get everything out, but that's the best I can do."

I grabbed at my phone and dialed, forgetting about covering myself. I saw his woman smile at me while she petted the brindle animal wagging his tail. The driver looked down at his watch to check the time and turned back toward the truck, another night in his life spent watching others lose part of theirs. "What's up, hun?" My dad was obviously asleep, and late-night phone calls were unusual, even when I was with Mike, so he must've realized the urgency.

"They're trying to take my car, Dad. They want my car."

I didn't feel I could call my dad when I left Mike. I'd pushed away my family after they showed little support for my relationship.

But now, my dad got out his credit card information and asked to speak to the driver.

"No, sir, you can't pay me now. I have to take the car. You can call the bank tomorrow and pay them, but the car is scheduled to be in Kansas City by then."

I heard my dad's voice rise as he asked the driver to put me back on the phone. He was louder but monotone.

"There's nothing we can do," he said. "Try to get some sleep and we'll take care of it in the morning."

"I'm sorry, Dad. I didn't know this was happening. I didn't know they would be here now."

"I know, hun. Goodnight."

I grabbed my car key out of my purse and walked the path to my driveway to check for valuables.

Two crumpled dollar bills were on the floorboard. I put them in my pocket and kept digging. A pen and a blanket from the backseat. My iPod was in the console.

A pipe and a dime sack were in the glove compartment. Mike must've stashed them there. I shoved them into the blanket and took the contents of my car into the house, dumping them on the couch. Back outside, I signed away my rights to the car and sat on the porch steps.

Was the man surprised by my appearance? I assumed repossessions only happened to long-bearded rednecks dressed in dirty wife beaters in sketchy trailer parks. Yet here I stood with exposed shoulders, a young blonde girl in suburbia having her first adult purchase taken away from her. Truth be told, I wasn't so different from those people in the trailer park. I couldn't afford to keep my shit and I'd loved a man who beat me. I was in the midst of a crisis, judging someone else, and I realized how petty humans can be.

He said little as he hooked my car to his truck.

"Things can always get better, ma'am," he said, before walking back to his truck to leave.

I watched as he drove away with my car, unable to move until he and it were out of sight. Once they were gone, I had no reason to stay outside. I looked down at the phone Mike's dad gave me. It was almost four o'clock in the morning. The sun would start to rise in an hour and I knew I'd be busy trying to clean up another mess. One I made for myself when I fell in love with the wrong guy.

Anger dried my mouth and I could feel my heartbeat in my temples. I locked the front door and turned off the lights.

Watson sat on the bed wagging his tiny black tail at me. It didn't matter to him whether I had a car or not, where we lived or how I dressed. So, I cried again, knowing my dad wouldn't accept my tears. He would call them weakness.

I reached deep into the blanket to extract the weed and pipe I found in my car.

I held them in my hand, fighting whether or not to smoke. I needed to calm down. I needed to escape. My life was falling apart now more than it had three days before. I wiped my sweaty palms against the comforter. Watson pushed his head under my hand and rolled onto his back, wagging his tail and hoping for affection. Coping wasn't going to be easy. If I didn't have a car, I couldn't get a job.

I sat at the edge of my dust-covered dresser and straddled the corner. I let my knees fall outward around it. This was just too hard.

Filling my lungs and stomach with air, I counted to four as I exhaled, sighing as the breath left my body. I already regretted what I was about to do. With one hand on the blue wall to my left, I wrapped my right hand around the front of the furniture and slammed my head into the edge of the dresser. And then I did it again. And again.

I stood, dizzy, realizing the physical pain did its job. I was numb to the torture in my head and heart.

I found a lighter inside my summer bag, packed the bowl full of the sticky buds and smoked enough weed to make everything else go away.

CHARLIE

I HEARD HER PULL into the empty driveway twenty minutes early. My youngest sister, Charlie, was off work and I needed her to drive me to my first job interview. My car was across the state at an auction. My dad couldn't pick it up until he got a loan for the asking price. Even then, I wouldn't be getting it back. He was going to sell it in hopes we could get our money back while salvaging a few points on his credit score since he'd co-signed my loan.

The interview was for a part-time teaching job at a Montessori preschool six miles away, and paid little more than minimum wage. I wouldn't earn enough to continue paying my mortgage, but smart spending would allow me to cover the utilities and buy groceries until the bank took my house. I knew it was inevitable, another reason my depression sank further. First my job. Then my car. My house was next.

Charlie walked in the front door while I finished applying a final coat of eyeliner to my left eyelid. Luckily, I kept my work wardrobe from my two years in teaching. It was nearly one hundred degrees outside, but the wool slacks were the only ones that fit my dwindling frame. I hardly ate. And couldn't really afford to either.

"You ready to go, 'Fina?"

I was ready to hibernate until the stress subsided. I turned around to look at her, attempting my first smile of the day.

"DJ wants to grab lunch while I'm waiting for you. His break starts at the same time as your interview, so I'll be back when you're done. Hopefully." She flicked her hair across her forehead and tucked it behind her ear, turning her head to the side so she could admire her profile.

It wasn't her fault I was miserable, but she was too young to understand I needed to hear about something other than her happiness. Or nothing at all. It was the first time in my life I wanted people to lie to my face and pretend they were as unhappy as me.

My dad adopted Charlie when she was sixteen, but she was a part of my family long before he signed the papers. Her brother, Dan, changed his last name to Bianco, too. He was eighteen when the adoption proceedings began, too old to be officially adopted. They were babies when my dad started dating their mom, my stepmom. Their common law marriage hit while I was in college, so they went to the courthouse and made it official one early August day.

I remembered seeing her for the first time on Halloween. Diane brought the kids trick or treating, pretending to be a friend of my dad's long before we knew they were a couple. Our houses were only fifteen minutes apart, but her blue ranch was already losing value in Spanish Lake. The city was crime-ridden and the people who still had the means fled in droves, mostly white. At the time, Charlie was two and Dan was four. I was nine. They walked in, wearing homemade pumpkin costumes, their cheeks as round as the orange fabric. I sat on the living room carpet with them, dividing and exchanging candy, while my dad and their mom flirted in the kitchen.

The scent of their coffee filled the living room and I could hear muffled outbursts of laughter coming from their direction. I was confused when my dad laughed with her, as though he hadn't laughed my entire childhood. But the kids kept me busy, attempting to take my Snickers bars when our parents' giggles stole my attention. I didn't have time to think about the significance of our unexpected guest.

"Do you live in a castle?" Charlie asked. Her legs circled the pile of gum and chocolate bar miniatures. Appropriate, maybe, because I thought I was elementary school royalty: a member of band, student council, choir, safety patrol and every other activity to distract me from my home life. I kept myself noticed and busy, a little distance between me and my family made me feel safer. I didn't do well with other people's pain because I always felt their suffering as though it was my own. When my parents divorced, the mixture of my guilt and their resentment for one another was too much.

Now, almost twenty years later, I wanted to do the same. "Let's do this," I said, turning away from the mirror and flipping off the bathroom light. "Anymore makeup and I'm going to look like Tammy Faye Baker."

She stared blankly in my direction and I realized the generation gap was larger than I assumed.

* * *

"It's not every day we get an applicant with such great experience," the director said.

I smiled, staring over her shoulder at the cluttered wall. I imagined the finger-paintings and photographs of smiling children laughed at my unhappiness. I couldn't display any hint of depression.

"You were an assistant director of a center and then moved on to get your education degree. It's impressive, 'Fina."

I wiped away tiny beads of sweat across my eyebrow. It was true. I was overqualified for the position, but I had to start making money. So I explained away the gaps in my employment, spinning lies about my sad past: I wanted to get back into education after spending a year working in the writing field. I wasn't sure if I was best suited for the young or big kids.

"I'm going to call your references. There's no reason to host another interview when we can't possibly pass on such great experience," she said, and then stood to guide me to the front door.

The guilt of my lies sank in as I walked toward Charlie's car. Or was I lying? I wasn't sure. Mike had done his best to make me second-guess everything I said and did. I blamed myself for every little thing that happened. If only I could turn around and explain the truth of my circumstances.

How do I tell someone I quit my full-time, salaried position to work for my boyfriend, who only wanted to alienate me so I had nothing good in my life? Then he stole my money, my dignity, and my future. And now I was left to question who was worse, the manipulator or me, the idiot who fell for it.

"How'd it go?" Charlie asked, as she pushed the passenger door open.

"It was fine. I'm ready for a nap." I slunk down further into the seat, hoping the director couldn't see me getting into someone else's car. We didn't talk the rest of the drive and I did my best to look away from her every time she tried.

"Are you sure you don't want my leftovers?" Charlie asked, pulling up to the curb next to my house. I could smell the sweetness of melted brown sugar.

She caught me staring down at the box, examining it and questioning whether or not I could humble myself to accept her help. "It's a sweet potato."

I searched for the door handle, blinded by my ego. "No. Thanks for the ride, Charlie," I said. I opened the door and hoped my insincerity wasn't obvious. My youngest sister, a recent high school graduate and part-time Dairy Queen worker, was better off than me.

I sat on the hardwood living room floor staring around at a house that used to hold so much promise. The walls were caving in around me now. Watson's whining at the front door saved me from staying on the floor for the rest of the night.

A LONG WAY FROM NORMAL

"READY TO GO, hun?" my dad asked.

It was four o'clock in the morning, the sun still underground. My dad picked me up for the four-hour trip to retrieve my car from Kansas City. The bank approved his loan application the day before, and even though it was unlikely the auction would sell my car so early in the day, I couldn't sit still the entire drive across the state. Once we got back, I would have to head to my first day of work. Reclaiming the car and beginning a new job, more so because of the circumstances, felt like huge progress.

"Be prepared, 'Fina. Auctions take the parts they want. It might be missing rims or a sound system."

The drive across Missouri provided two lanes of boredom, since my dad and I never conversed for long. My mind wandered back to my last Kansas City trip, visiting college friends. We laughed and drank and ate, carelessly predicting where each of us would be in in ten years. This time, it was totally different, and I was glad they couldn't see me. I was the opposite of successful.

The lot at the auction was a checkerboard of new-looking cars. I could see hundreds of vehicles from the passenger side of my dad's car. It was too much for me, all that misfortune.

"Do you want to give them the money?" My dad pressed his foot on the brake and looked directly at me, waiting for a response.

"Why would I do that, Dad?" My question cut through the awkward conversation. He lifted his eyebrow, as if it was the first time he ever heard me speak.

"Because this is your mess, 'Fina," he said, looking away from me, absorbing the same cars I refused to see.

* * *

My dad drove the Bug home. My mess was his now and if he had it his way, someone else's soon. Dangerous to other drivers, I stared at my car while he drove it home, my vision blurred by the usual tears. For four hours, I watched the yellow car cruise across the state, back toward my hometown, a mocking reminder of my failure.

* * *

The scent of bleach overwhelmed my nose when I walked into the daycare center, but the strong waft of messy diapers took over halfway through my shift. I had to remind myself I needed this job. At least I worked with the older kids who could wipe their own asses.

"What's your story?" the classroom teacher said, "Are you in college?"

"No, I was a high school teacher."

She walked away, wiping down the table surface with bleach-water. Across the room in lunch-stained pants, a kid ran free with a booger falling from her left nostril.

"Girl, you're a long way from normal."

SIX MONTHS AFTER SUNSET

WORKING AT THE DAYCARE daycare had a few good things. The first, and most relevant, after successfully working part-time for one month, the director – a job I held while in college – asked me to apply for the full-time, co-lead teacher position in one of the rooms. After a simple interview, I was hired. I would only make $9 an hour, but it was a raise and more hours. Plus, if it worked out, I would have the chance to get health insurance, a necessity I hadn't had since my last teaching position.

Second, I could work less hours at the Shack. The owners allowed me to come back to work after bailing on them when I moved to Louisiana. While Mike hadn't shown his face in a while, he continued leaving business cards and pens, marking his territory. Spending any time there meant I ran the risk of seeing him, and I switched shifts so he couldn't reenter my life. Last, the other co-lead teacher and I became closer and closer. She didn't know about my abusive past. We enjoyed ordering food and dishing about celebrities and her on-and-off-again boyfriend, and she distracted me from the life I was trying to leave behind.

Her name was Scarlett. Originally from Orlando, Florida, she moved to St. Louis to attend Logan Chiropractic College. At least, that's what she told everyone, but the truth was that she moved here for her high school boyfriend, turned fiancé, who wanted to be a chiropractor. Scarlett wasn't sure what she wanted to do, so she followed him across the country and into a college major. It didn't take her long to decide she didn't want to be a chiropractor, but it took her even less time to realize she didn't like her boyfriend.

When they arrived in St. Louis, Marcus became more and more possessive, and ended up beating her pretty bad. So, after a year in a new state, she had to decide if she wanted to move home or stay. She fell in love with the city, and fortunately for her, fell in love with another chiropractic student. She chased one guy here and found another one before she decided to move home. It became clear her relationship with him wasn't perfect, either. He couldn't say I love you, and she couldn't give up on the possibility he might. So she stayed with him. It was better than the alternative: moving home defeated or staying with a controlling, abusive man.

Scarlett had long, red hair I envied. Even though I stopped cutting off my hair after I left Mike, wisps of hair were only brushing my jawbone by Thanksgiving. Seeing her hair made me wish I'd never cut mine off, and I decided to grow it out again. I'd do the exact opposite of what Mike wanted. Hearing her talk about her relationship problems made it easy for me to avoid men, and it also made me realize we weren't all that different. She loved her abusive boyfriend through thick and thin, only wanting to fix him by loving him harder. Outsiders never understood what this was like, and finding someone who did – even if she didn't know my story yet – made changing diapers and cleaning up puke bearable.

The frustrating part about working with toddlers was how much it made me miss my teenage students. When I left teaching, I never anticipated wanting to go back. After spending months ghostwriting in a cubicle, my career came to a close (due to lack of customers). I often found myself dreaming of returning to a classroom. A preschool wasn't good enough. After a few months working there, even after gaining a new friend, I decided it was time to start thinking about returning to the classroom.

* * *

It was almost Christmas, and time to strengthen my application packet. Most school districts began posting teaching openings in March for the following school year. Included in said packet is the standard resume and letter of intent, however, in education you're also required to send three letters of recommendation to any hiring district. *This wouldn't be too troublesome, except I hadn't taught the previous year and wouldn't start a job until I'd already been out of the classroom for two years.*

Immediately, my mind raced to the interview stage. How the hell would I explain my sabbatical? I planned to sugarcoat the pile-of-poo reason – *that my boyfriend convinced me my talent wasn't being utilized and I'd be better off writing* – by saying I needed time away to realize exactly where I should be: in the classroom.

I hoped the districts would buy it. *Lucky for me, Scarlett had already gone home for the holidays and the daycare had a substitute all week. That meant I could work without listening to a guilt trip from her. She didn't want me to leave the preschool. I couldn't imagine staying any longer.*

First, I updated my resume. Then I contacted the administrators who wrote my letters of recommendation to explain I was going to begin the job hunt as soon as hiring season rolled around. This would only be problematic for one recommendation: the principal of the high school who was devastated when I decided to walk away from teaching.

She was pissed. In fact, my last two months teaching were spent with daily reminders that I was making a huge mistake. On the days she wasn't attempting to coax me into reconsidering the decision, she ignored me. In the end, the relationship became awkward enough that I avoided conversations with her altogether. It wasn't exactly the ideal work environment.

There I sat, in front of my computer, with Gmail open and her email address plugged in, without a fucking clue what to say. I knew I needed to be honest. I told her I was once again bit with the teaching bug. I explained I was hoping she could update my letter of recommendation so I could to begin applying when teaching positions started opening up again. And then I waited.

Sarafina,

I must say I was surprised by your email. The last time I heard from you, you were becoming a writing superstar and were just mentioned in The Post. *However, I'd be lying if I said I didn't know you'd get back into teaching. The connection you made with kids was remarkable. I knew you'd miss them…miss it.*

I'd be happy to update your letter of recommendation. I don't have it saved on my computer so, if you wouldn't mind, could you send me a copy so I can update and sign it?

Just out of curiosity, what was the final straw that led you to this moment?

Take care,

Beth

Beth not only responded, but she complimented me. When I started teaching, she was my role model, maybe the best role model in the world of education. A true, passionate and caring administrator, she took me under her wing and molded me into an exemplary teacher. For her kindness, I was forever indebted. She was part of the reason I wanted to get back into teaching.

Beth,

I've been missing the classroom for several months and, to be honest, I do miss the kids. Thank you so much for all of your support and guidance. You created a monster inside of me. It's time to get back into the classroom and do my thang.

Thanks again for helping me out with my letter of recommendation.

It just so happens I found a job opening online for January and I might apply (even though it's three weeks away from the start date). I figure it'll be good to get my feet wet. I doubt I'll get the job, but if I get an interview, it'll be good practice.

This means the world to me,
Sarafina

I didn't hear back for several days.

It was nap-time at the preschool and all of the snotty rug-rats were sleeping when I received another email from Beth. I grabbed my phone to check my email.

Sarafina,

Interesting turn of events. We now have an English position open that would start in January. Want to talk about it? Call the school and we can set up a time (either via phone or in person).

Looking forward to it,
Beth

My heart was pounding. I sent a gasp through the room so loudly one of the babies woke up. After patting them back into a coma, I reread the email.

We now have an English position open that would start in January. Want to talk about it?

Life was headed in the right direction. Sure, the position wasn't exactly mine, but if Beth was willing to mention it, there was a damn good chance I'd be back in my old school teaching again within a few weeks. I pinched myself a few times. Yep, it was happening.

Something else made it almost impossible to believe this day was real. I received a call from my realtor the same unbelievable day. Instead of a foreclosure, I would only have a short sale on my credit score. The closing was four weeks away.

Two days later, I was offered the gig. Three weeks after that, I would start. I'd have some of the same students, the same principal and a great staff of people to welcome me back. While I hadn't anticipated being back in the classroom until the following fall, I had every reason to accept the position and start in three weeks.

MOVING OUT

CHRISTMAS CAME AND went, and so did my twenty-seventh birthday days later; then New Years. On January 2, 2010, exactly two years after the damn train, I moved out of my house and into a rental property near the school, in a tiny rural town made up of mostly farmers, a few meth heads, small families, single mothers, and the rare couple who refused to leave behind their impoverished hometown.

My dad, my brother Dan, and a few friends (Scarlett, Topher, and Val) came to help me pack the rest of my belongings into a U-Haul and drive me west toward my future. Even though I spent hours working on packing my belongings, we spent the majority of the day picking up the toiletries, canned goods, hangers, and trinkets left scattered about. I felt good leaving. I wanted out of Magnolia too. Even though Sunset was where he'd tried to kill me, Magnolia was where the abuse started, where I was reminded of him daily: by the train, by the still-broken window and my front yard view of his office.

Every item I packed reminded me of Mike. I decided to keep the boots from our second date but trash the necklace from our trip to Springfield. Staring as my dad and brother took my dresser out to the moving van, I remembered slamming my head into the side of it over and over again.

With five people pulling me up and out toward a better life, smiling because they didn't understand, I couldn't ignore the space that grew every time they thought I should too. Sure, this was a new start. It was also the moment I lost my house. A short sale sounded better to them, but it was a failure, and I had to start over.

My dad handed me his credit card and asked me to stop on the way to pick up soda and beer for everyone. I picked up two thirty-packs of Bud Light, a few Cokes and a pack of Marlboro Lights. I opened a beer and drove down the highway smoking cigarettes, and drinking while listening to the radio signal fade in and out as I got closer to my exit.

They were backing the truck into the gravel driveway when I made a right on Miller and passed the white ranch-style house on the corner someone turned into a funeral home. Before I found the rental, I had only been on Miller once, and it was for a visitation in the makeshift mortuary. My student passed away from a brain injury after she was ejected from a car, just a day after her husband – her high school sweetheart – returned from a tour overseas. He was nineteen. She was twenty. At that point, it was the saddest funeral I'd ever attended. Especially since people were smoking inside.

The uptight side of me thought it was disrespectful to my student, a reminder I wasn't the girl who thought that way anymore. Because while I continued, remembering my criticisms, I was drinking and driving. At least I could see the hypocrisy. I parked a few houses down the day they buried my student, on the north side of the street, almost directly in front of the house I was moving into. I smiled a little then, thinking about irony. A little more than a year before, I told myself I would never let my life get so bad as to have a funeral in a tiny space, full of people who didn't respect my body enough to smoke outside. And, now, I was moving onto the street where I made myself that promise. Smoking was nowhere near as harmful as my ex-boyfriend.

I crushed the beer can and hid it under my seat.

* * *

Discarded pieces of Pergo sat on top of the dusty, stained floor. The walls were covered in words scrawled in red crayon and marker up to my waist. The writing made its way from the living room to the dining room, then down the hallway into my bedroom. It made sense the rent was cheap.

Denny, my former student arrested because of the disassembled rifle in his car, helped his mom keep up with her rental properties in the area. He heard I was looking for a place to stay, so he sent me a Facebook message to tell me the old tenant's lease expired and they weren't renewing. I was welcome to move in for $400 a month. Denny's sentence at juvenile was up, and he worked his ass off to prove his tiny mistake (tinkering with an antique gun) wouldn't define the rest of his life. The kid had it together now and I was proud to see him succeed after adversity: the bitterness of life joined us together, even if he didn't know it.

Rent was only one third of the cost of my mortgage, a price I could *finally* afford. Denny told me they needed to do some cleaning and conditioning before it would be ready, but it was clear they weren't done with either of those things while I stood in the living room. We stashed boxes around the clean edges of each room, and spent some time cleaning up the areas I would need to use: the bedroom, kitchen and bathroom.

The oven gave off a gas smell. And as soon as I tried to move the old refrigerator back into its place, I noticed an unmarked bottle of yellow alcohol stashed between the copper coils. I moved it back and forth until it was free, and realized it wasn't alcohol. I could smell cleaner inside of it. *Why was there cleaner stashed under the refrigerator?* At least – at some point – somebody tried to clean this place.

My brother walked into the kitchen, holding a shoebox I'd packed earlier in the week. Topher and Val followed him, giggling as they watched him hand me the box. Buzzing in my hand, it hadn't been vibrating when I packed. Now, the tiny bullet inside had clearly been turned on during our forty minute trip. Dan handed it to me graciously and walked away without another word, Topher and Val still standing there, still laughing. Thankfully, the trashed house and the last two years of my life kept me occupied enough I couldn't remember what embarrassment felt like. That's when I remembered Mike saying, *every woman had a vibrator anyway*, and threw the entire shoe-box away without looking inside.

* * *

Every creak of the floorboards and punch of the heat kicking on freaked me out. Being alone in the new house for the first time was terrifying, a constant reminder I didn't know the house well enough to escape if I needed. At my old house, and on Sunset, I'd had escape routes drawn in my head for the bad days. Here, if anything were to happen I wouldn't know how to get out.

I stayed at the house, cleaning and unpacking as much as I could. School started in two days and I needed to get as much ready as possible. Denny's mom called to check on me, and she was surprised when she heard about the walls and floors, plus the gas smell and the strange items I found in the kitchen. She promised to send Denny over the next day. And she hired a woman to come in and clean the house, top to bottom. She also said I could paint the house instead of paying the first month's rent. I was excited about all of those things happening, even though I couldn't take off my shoes yet.

I closed the bedroom door so Watson couldn't roam through the mess. He was curled into a ball on my mattress, comfortably sleeping as I tried to salvage the folds in my T-shirts instead of refolding all of them. The ceilings were high and only one red light worked in the light fixture, so I left the hallway and bathroom lights on.

"This is it, buddy. It's just you and me." I said.

Watson rolled onto his side and relaxed his belly, pushing it out against the comforter as he sighed loudly.

"At least somebody feels like they're at home."

I dropped the last bit of my laundry onto the top of the dresser and fell backwards onto the bed. The bedroom was tiny enough that I didn't have to worry. I could fall anywhere in it and land on my mattress. Watson lifted his head and put it on my stomach. He sighed again, sending warm breath across my belly. I petted his head and listened to his whimpers.

"Welcome to your new home, baby."

I grabbed my phone and signed into Facebook, taking a break from my to-do list. No matter how much I finished that night, the house wasn't going to be ready. I drifted in and out of consciousness, laughing about my brother, my vibrator, and the fucking mess in the living room. Unexpected, extra stress was funny, even if it was inconvenient. I sat up in bed, staring up at the red light bulb left behind by the former renter, contemplating which lights to leave on and switch off. I didn't move, deciding to ignore them.

Simple decisions took longer than before. I didn't want the unknown household sounds to keep me awake. I was scared of everything, the slightest ping of the heater or a creak in the door sent me into a catatonic state: rocking back and forth, scratching my thighs until exhaustion set in. If leaving the lights on prevented me from inflicting pain, I was willing to pay a little extra to the electric company.

It was the strangest moment to hear someone trying to break into my house. Sitting up on the bed, fighting off sleep, I realized I was delusional. Nobody knew where I was or who was living in the property. I convinced myself I heard the walls buckling to the cold January night, and I laid my head back on the pillow. I tapped my right hand on Watson's butt over and over, counting each tap to keep myself distracted from the fear settling hard on my chest. I made it to twenty before I heard it again. In the back of the house, under the carport, a push against the door, like Mike used to do when I locked myself in a room.

Watson jumped at the last sound, proving I didn't imagine the noise. He leapt from the bed and ran through the kitchen, straight to the back door, where he barked until the pounding stopped. I screamed his name and dialed 911, running for the bedroom door to hold it shut in case someone got in. *Had he found me?* "Nine-one-one. What's your emergency," the operator said.

"Someone's breaking in my house. It's three-eleven Miller. Please, I'm here alone and it's my first night."

"Hang tight, ma'am, we have an officer in route. The city's station is closed for the night so we're sending someone from county. Can you hear anyone in the house?"

Watson was back at the bedroom door, crying for me to let him in. I sat still, listening for footsteps or any sign of a person. "No, it's quiet now. But please send someone. Please don't leave me here alone." I choked back sobs as the operator reassured me a car was on its way. "I'm supposed to start teaching tomorrow." Panic and rage tightening the muscles in my hands, I wanted to cut myself to refocus the pain.

* * *

The first officer to arrive was off-duty, the chief who lived in town and heard my call on the radio.

"You'll have to come out of your room and let me in," he said through the front door. I yelled back. "But what if someone's in here?"

"If they're in there with you I'll be sure to bust the door in. You have to come out and let me help you."

I ran through the house, kicking up dust as I ran across the busted floors to the front door. Nobody chased me except Watson.

"Well then, tell me what happened and we'll get you squared

away."

The chief was nice enough, a middle-aged man with kind eyes and a perfectly symmetrical smile. He walked each room of the house, inspecting it for signs of someone breaking and entering.

"Did your landlord tell you what happened here?"

My stomach dropped into my butt. "No, but they gave me a good deal."

"Well, the guy who lived here used to cook meth, we think. And his wife left him so he held her hostage in that room." He pointed toward the dining room. "It took us two days to get her out."

"I'm not sure this story is helping me."

"No, but what would help you is if you took that red light out of the fixture. You see, that means you're cooking. I bet your friend who showed up here was looking for a fix." Just as he explained I'd inadvertently drawn an addict's attention to the house, the front door opened and two more county cops walked in. "We're back here, boys," the chief said.

"This here is Miss Bianco. She's going to be teaching at Millerville High School and somebody tried to break in tonight. Not exactly the best welcome, as you can imagine."

I rummaged around the house looking for my belongings to head a half an hour down the highway and sleep on my dad's couch. A short, fat officer younger than me walked into my path.

"Oh, so you're a teacher," he said.

I looked up at him, holding a bra and dress in one hand. "Yes, at the high school."

"Well they sure didn't make teachers like you in my day," he said, tilting his cap toward me.

I stared back at the chief who chuckled before realizing I was angry. "All right, boys, go on ahead and head out. I'll take care of Miss Bianco from here."

PROMISES

I STILL OWED my mortgage company, even though I signed a release when the short sale went through. I received a collections letter, demanding I pay more than $10,000 on a loan modification they approved. Basically, they pushed back my overdue payments and put them on the end of the life of the loan. That meant it didn't count toward my original mortgage. Every day I didn't pay, the secondary loan was accruing interest. Add that to what I owed my dad for the moving van, what I owed Topher for my utility payments, and the back bills on everything else.

The therapy I so badly needed was off the table.

I made it through my first six months back in the classroom and was offered a contract to continue teaching at the high school the following year. Scarlett moved in with me about a month after I moved into the house on Miller. She found a job at a local daycare center, providing in-home assessments for parents. I refused to teach summer school, knowing the work I needed to do on myself was more than enough to keep me busy. Plus, I had a steady paycheck coming in once a month. It was time for a break.

I left Mike almost eleven months before and, even though I did my best to distance myself, the nightmares and anxiety still beat me. Searching for ways to self-sooth, I ended up on WordPress.

Username: UndeniablyUnidentifable

I sat in the dark at my roommate Scarlett's desktop computer staring at the black keyboard, hoping words would come easy, like they did when I started ghostwriting. I created a Nirvana station on Pandora. Then another for Patti Griffin. And John Mayer. "Daughters" was the third song to play on the third station I created. By the time it was over, I wrote this:

I can't promise you'll love every post. I probably won't either. In a world so eager to bring everyone to their knees, I think it's safe to say my identity will remain as anonymous as possible. I have a budding career as an educator to think about. Teachers don't have sex, sleep or drink.

__Why would you care to read beyond this post?__ I have a dirty little closet to clean and a perspective that's fairly unique. I've got a brain most people wish they could pick a little more than I allow. I'll entertain you, push you to see the gray areas and question all motives (including my own). It's real, raw and flawed. That's life. This one happens to be mine. Welcome to it.

It was enough for the night.

Two posts later, I wrote about the whistle of the train.

Four posts after that, I wrote this:

At the ripe age of twenty-six, I found myself in a full-blown abusive relationship.

Almost exactly a year ago today, I left Ike for good. For one and a half years, he wrapped his physical and mental manacles around me and then sucked the life and breath out of me (HP Dementor style).

He promised to change. He did.

He started doing cocaine, smoking excessive amounts of marijuana. He stole money from me and drank every night. He'd leave for thirty-six hours at a time on one of his benders. I'm sure he was unfaithful, but infidelity doesn't hold a candle to the other pain he inflicted.

He convinced me to quit teaching. He convinced me I was worthless without him. He belittled my abilities unless he was somehow attached to the achievement. Ike made one-sided demands of my time and effort, but never reciprocated.

At his best, he was the man I fell in love with: charming, passionate, loving and supportive. At his worst, he was a disgusting monster. I was tripped, choked, insulted and broken down.

At times, I knew the abuse was coming. He'd go to my purse, find my cell phone and smash it into tiny pieces. Because the bruises and blood were enough that he knew I'd be too embarrassed to leave and find another phone.

Ike was smart. My wounds always resembled some injury that could have been accidental or self-inflicted. He would sweep my feet out from under me so I fell in conveniently dangerous places (near stairs or by glass). He would stand over me so I couldn't get up and if I tried, he would violently push me back to the floor, laughing.

Why didn't I leave?

My income as a freelance writer was minuscule. My self-esteem vanished. I was so alienated from friends and family, I didn't think I had anywhere to turn. I left everything and everyone for him. He had me exactly where he wanted me.

Alone.

I needed him.

Little pieces of my life shifted into place as I wrote. And I found myself sending Google docs of the drafts to friends to see if they approved. I was unsure of my voice, unable to tell if what I wrote was any good. I wrote in the dark every night, listening to whatever Pandora chose. And I called him Ike because it fit.

The catharsis was the best therapy I could afford.

* * *

One thing I learned from Mike was how to promote myself online. He was a fan of Seth Godin and Gary Vaynerchuk. Of Purple Cows and Blue Oceans. I laughed out loud at the desk, waking Scarlett who was sleeping in her bedroom. All of the bullshit he forced me to read was going to come in handy.

First, I found an old picture of myself I took for an ex-boyfriend in the dark phase of my life. I had dyed my hair the darkest brown my stylist would allow with my fair complexion. I was wearing a tight navy blue cotton shirt with a sequenced bow hanging off the left shoulder, covering my shoulder blade and left breast. I wanted to look like a pin-up on the day of my photo shoot.

Sam, my older sister, came over and curled my shoulder length hair before brushing the curls out and spraying to hold the one strong curl left in the layer that accentuated my cheekbones. She used bronzer to define my jawline and plumped my thick lips with red stain and clear, heavy, lip gloss.

In the original picture, I looked up and out of the frame, strong and curious. But in blogging, fear kept me from sharing my entire face. I just couldn't afford for him to find me. So I cropped it just above my nostrils, only half of my face showing, and called myself Sarafina, the name my grandpa lovingly called my sister when we were kids. I was jealous of her nickname, wanting him to give me an Italian first name too. I took her nickname for myself and used it as my penname.

Then it dawned on me. What the entire blog would be about. How desperately I wanted to heal from this. My future. 'Fina's future. I changed my username to Future4Fina, to mimic the name I would use on Twitter.

I'M STILL BREATHING

IT'S BEEN FIVE years since I started my blog. A few months after it began, a reader contacted me with a detailed list of non-profits and free services for abuse survivors. Once I found out I could get the help I needed, I never looked back.

It's a story in and of itself, and one I hope to share when the time is right.

In July of 2014, I graduated from abuse therapy, three years after I started. Since then, I've moved my blog, just like the rest of my life, to another location: a symbolic shift between life before and after trauma therapy.

I could've told the rest of my story here, including my reinvention and rehabilitation. I could have told you the PTSD is nearly gone and I met a man, now my husband, who loved me through my nightmare. But sharing the good allows people who don't understand abuse to continue on without understanding it.

"What she went through was terrible," they say, "but look how happy she is now."

And they completely miss the point, overlooking the trauma and sadness and focusing on a silver-lining humanity deserves: happiness.

Abuse changes parts of you that were whole before, and rebuilds old fears into new traumas.

Abuse doesn't end when we leave. It haunts us, saturating every aspect of our lives until we're finally able to rid ourselves of the aftermath. It's not fair we were subjected to the torture, and it's not fair people choose to ignore the truth of abuse – that anyone can fall victim – because ignoring it makes them feel safer.

My hope for my readers is simple: that you find yourself in a place to speak out about the injustices you face. Our stories don't define us, but they shape where we head. Sometimes that's a good thing. Sometimes it's the worst. It's not about how you got here or why you stayed, it's about why it shouldn't have happened. About them: the abuser and their sickness. The aftermath and its impact.

As I self-published the original version of *The House on Sunset* I was astounded at how deceitful I felt after survivors reached out. They thanked me for my brutal honesty and raw depiction of my relationship. Suddenly, their comments of "we don't feel alone anymore," made me feel as if I was lying to them, the people who understand exactly where I've been. If they're brave enough to come forward and share their stories with me, then why couldn't I share my face?

Sarafina served her purpose when I needed her, protecting me from my abuser and my employer. Teachers can't have real lives so I knew what I wrote could get me in trouble, and I thought writing under a penname would be the shield I needed. Now, it's become the opposite of that: an unnecessary rift between myself and others, and so I write this, weeks before the second edition lands on Amazon, hopeful you'll all accept me as myself. Lindsay Fischer, the real woman who survived the life bled onto these pages. A now thirty-something who's ready to reclaim the life that was given to me, by refusing to hide.

Why?

Because there is life after abuse. This is mine.

There are no more secrets.

ABUSE HOTLINES

If you or a loved one needs help leaving an abusive relationship or suffers the aftermath of violence, there are worldwide organizations ready to help. The list I've included is not exhaustive, but a starting point in the journey to recovery.

Domestic Violence National Services in the United States

The National Domestic Violence Hotline
1-800-799- HELP (7233)
National Coalition Against Domestic Violence
National Network to End Domestic Violence
National Resource Center on Domestic Violence
Rape, Abuse, & Incest National Network (RAINN)

International Organization Resources

American Domestic Violence Crisis Line (Americans living overseas)
Domestic Violence & Incest Resource Centre (Australia)
Hot Peach Pages-(Worldwide List of Agencies Against Domestic Violence)
UNIFEM (United Nations Development for Women)
Women's Aid (United Kingdom)
Women's Link Worldwide (Western Europe and Latin America)

There's also a secret Facebook group available to survivors of domestic violence, one where survivors are able to share their struggles and lift up one another. If you are interested in enrolling in the group, I have to add you. Please friend me on Facebook first, and then send me a private message. Once you have done this, I will add you to our safe place. I'm also available on my fan page here.

*Because the group will be secret (not closed) nobody can search for it on Facebook. I have done this so we all remain safe and are comfortable sharing our stories. This will not be a place to post images of your abuse, but you are welcome to share your story. Out of respect for everyone included, all at different places in their journey, we will do our best to keep triggering information off the page.

#DomesticViolenceChat
Please join me, @Linsfischer, every Sunday afternoon (3pm EST) and Monday night (9pm EST) on Twitter for our weekly chat. To join, just search for the hashtag to follow the conversation. Then, when you're ready, use it to chime in. All survivors are welcome.

Read more about my rehabilitation and advocacy work at http://survivorswillbeheard.com

Made in the USA
Lexington, KY
16 March 2019